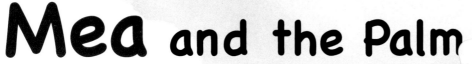

Mea and the Palm Flowers

Meirina Soe and Wini Boenadhi

together with

Ice Tede Dara and Geneviève Duggan

Edited by Sandra Sardjono

TRACING
PATTERNS
FOUNDATION

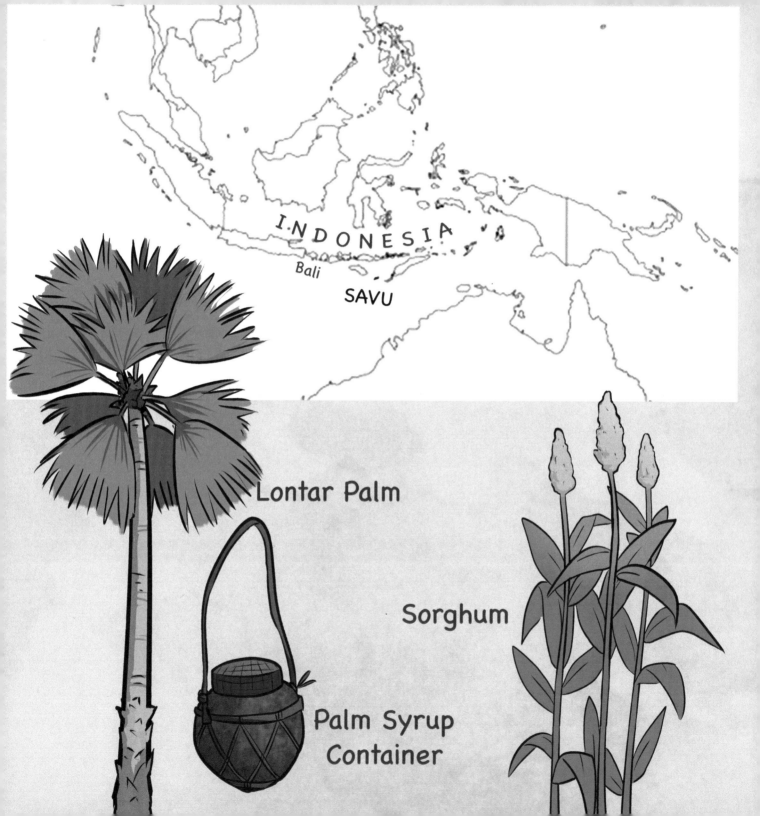

INDONESIA

Bali

SAVU

Lontar Palm

Sorghum

Palm Syrup
Container

Savu Island

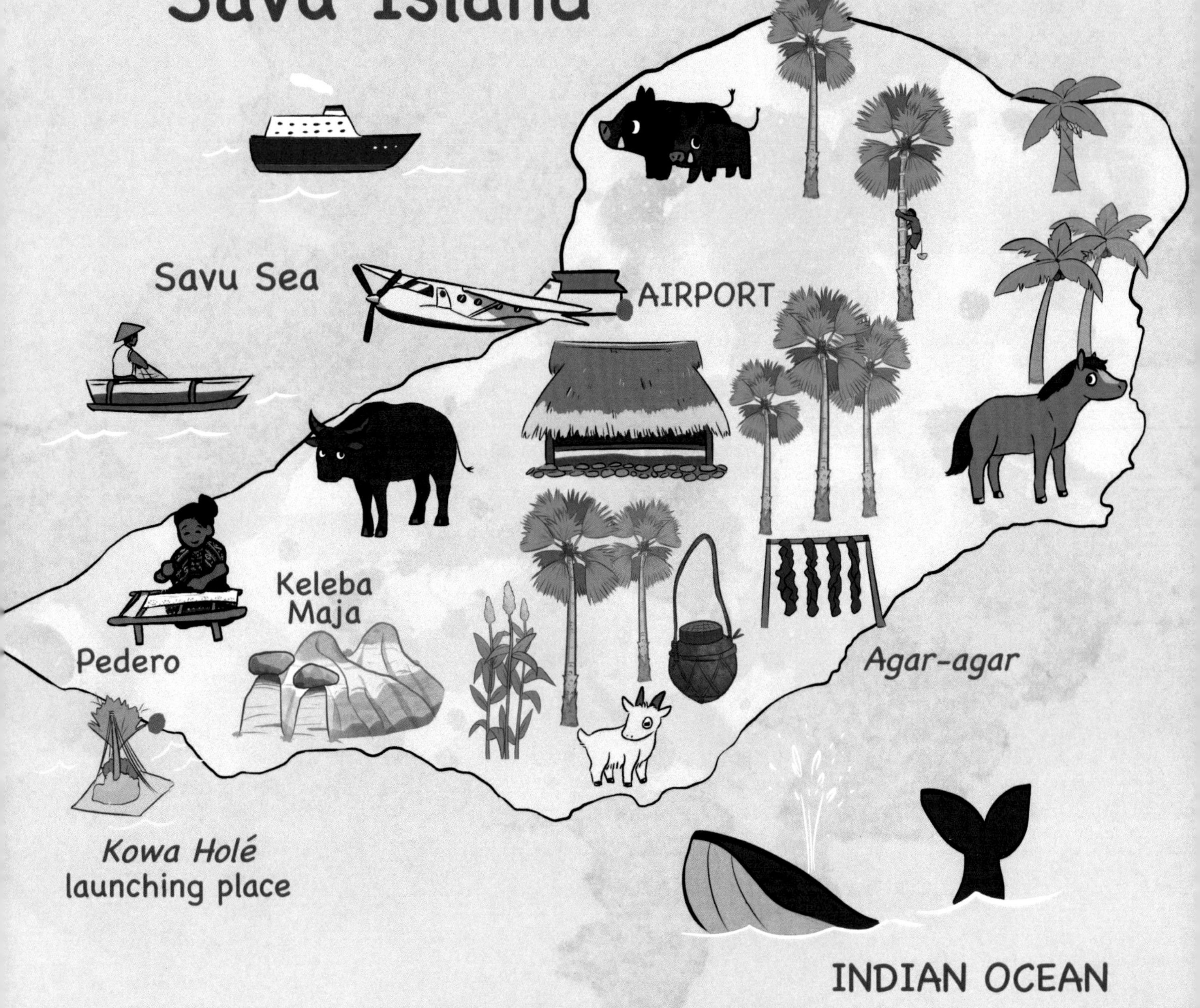
Savu Sea
AIRPORT
Keleba Maja
Pedero
Agar-agar
Kowa Holé launching place
INDIAN OCEAN

On the island of Savu, there are two large groups of people called the Big Palm Flowers and the Small Palm Flowers. They are named after flowers of palm trees, which have many uses in the daily lives in Savu. Each group comprises many families.

On the southwest tip of the island lies a small village called Pedero. Women in this village are expert at weaving a special cloth called *ikat*. They grow the cotton themselves, spin it into thread, tie and dye the thread, and weave it into cloth. Each family has special *ikat* patterns that are connected to the family's own histories.

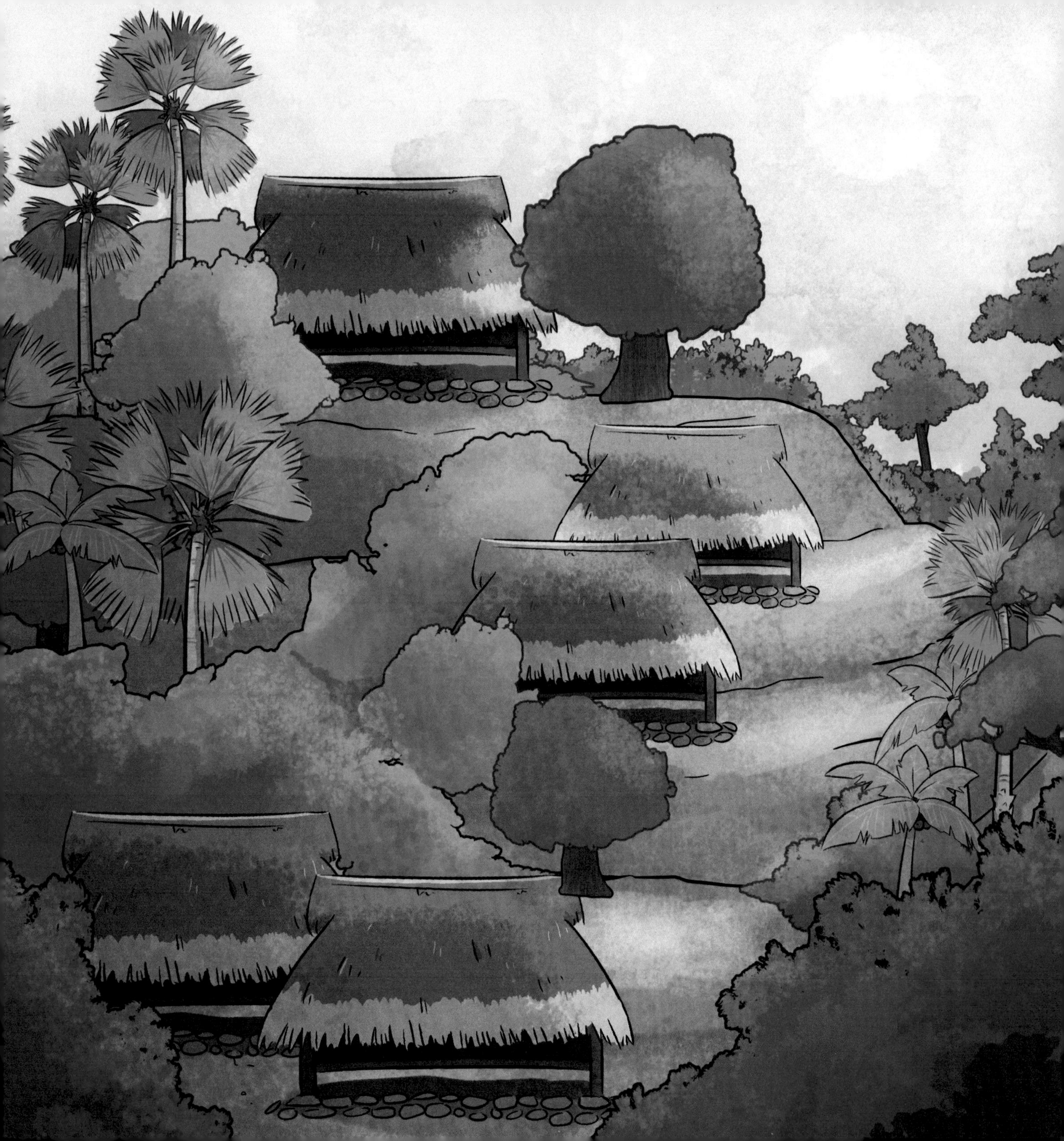

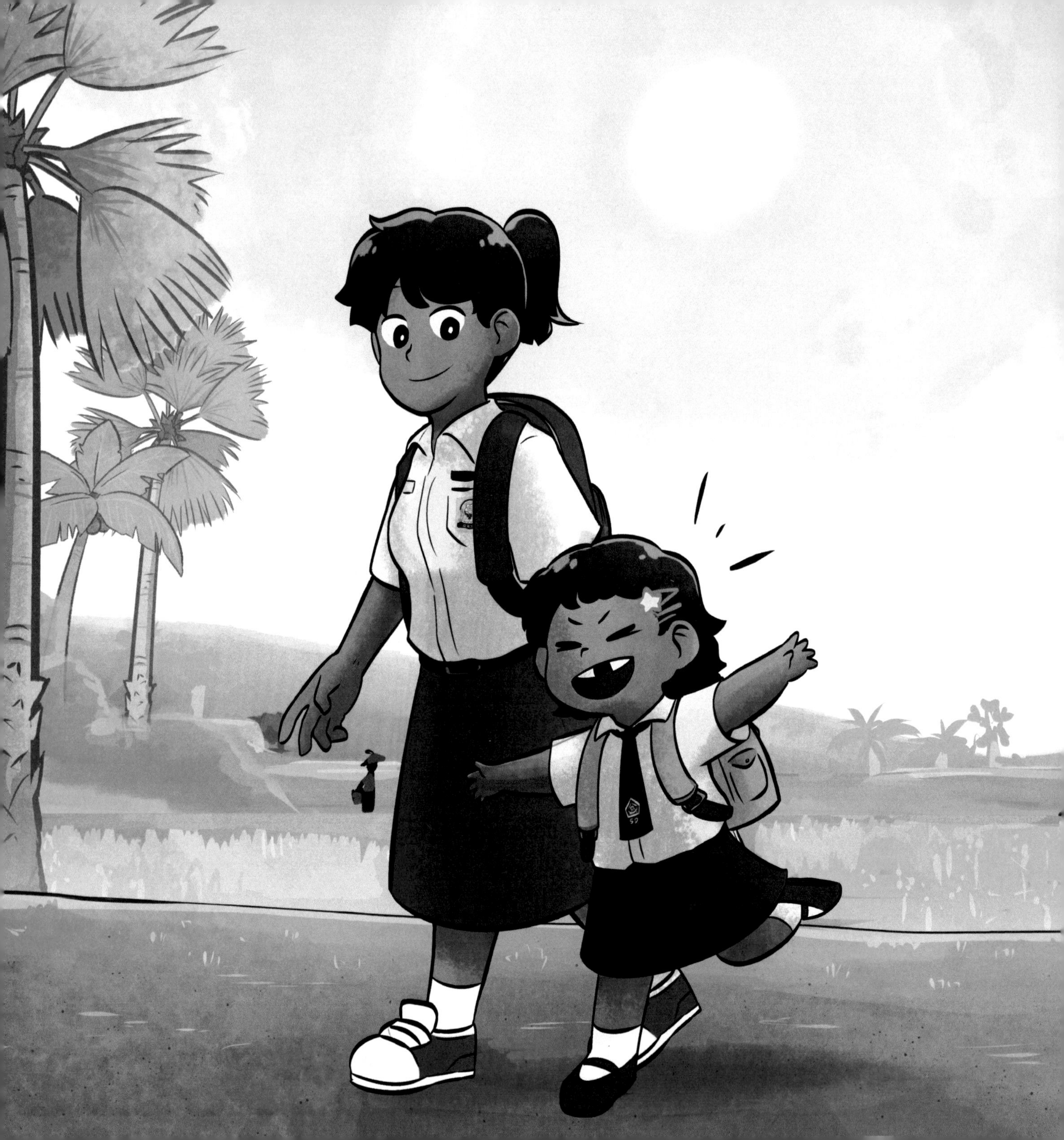

A little girl named Mea lives in Pedero Village.
Mea means "red" in the Savunese language.
Her family belongs to the Small Palm Flowers.

Mea loves her walk to school every morning
with her big sister and their dog.
They walk by many sorghum and rice fields,
vegetable gardens, and palm trees.

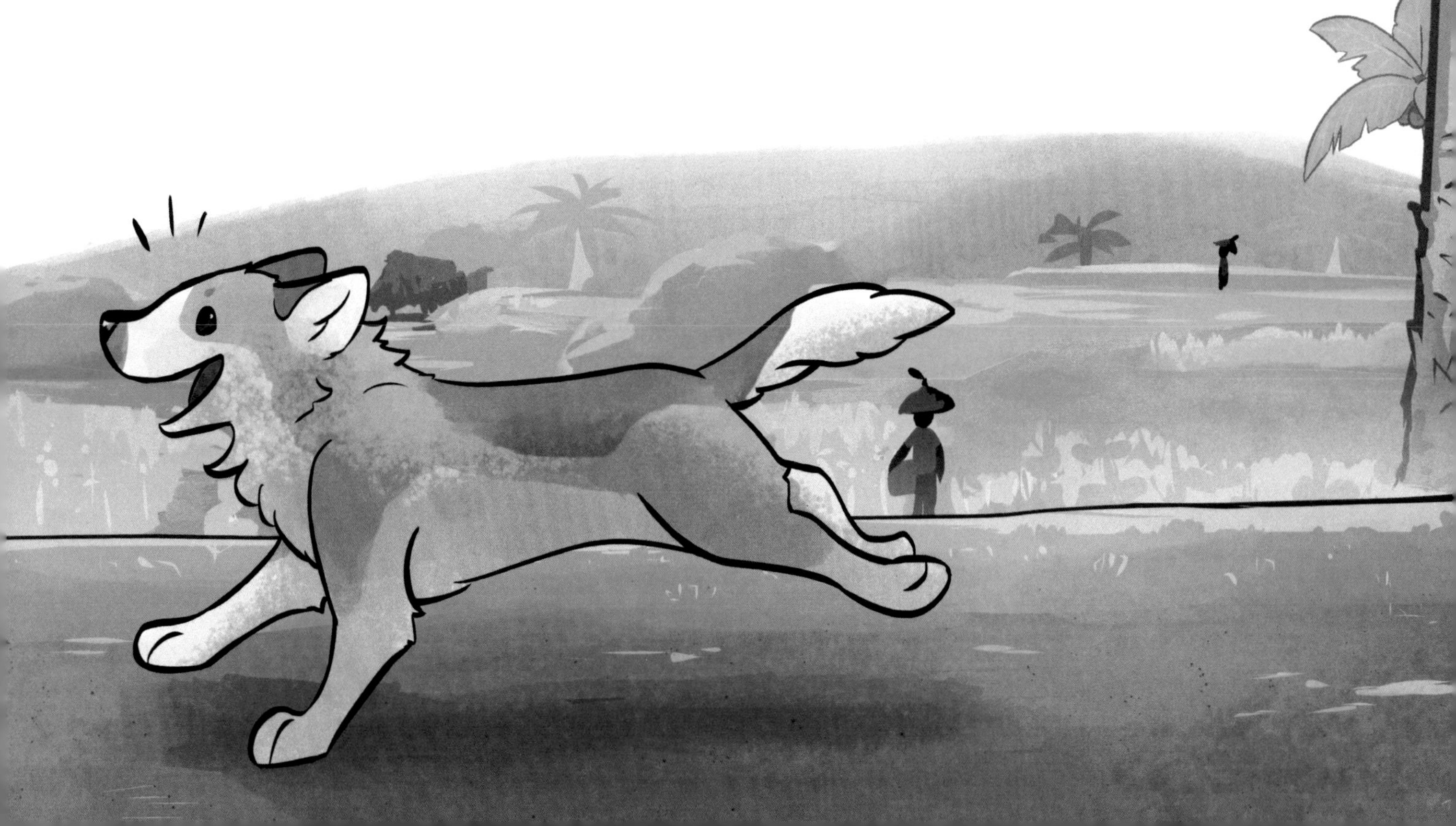

Today, people in the village seemed busier than usual. "What is going on?" Mea wondered.

Mea came across women working in the rice field. They were bending down to cut ears of rice. Mea liked their pointy hats, which are made of palm leaves.

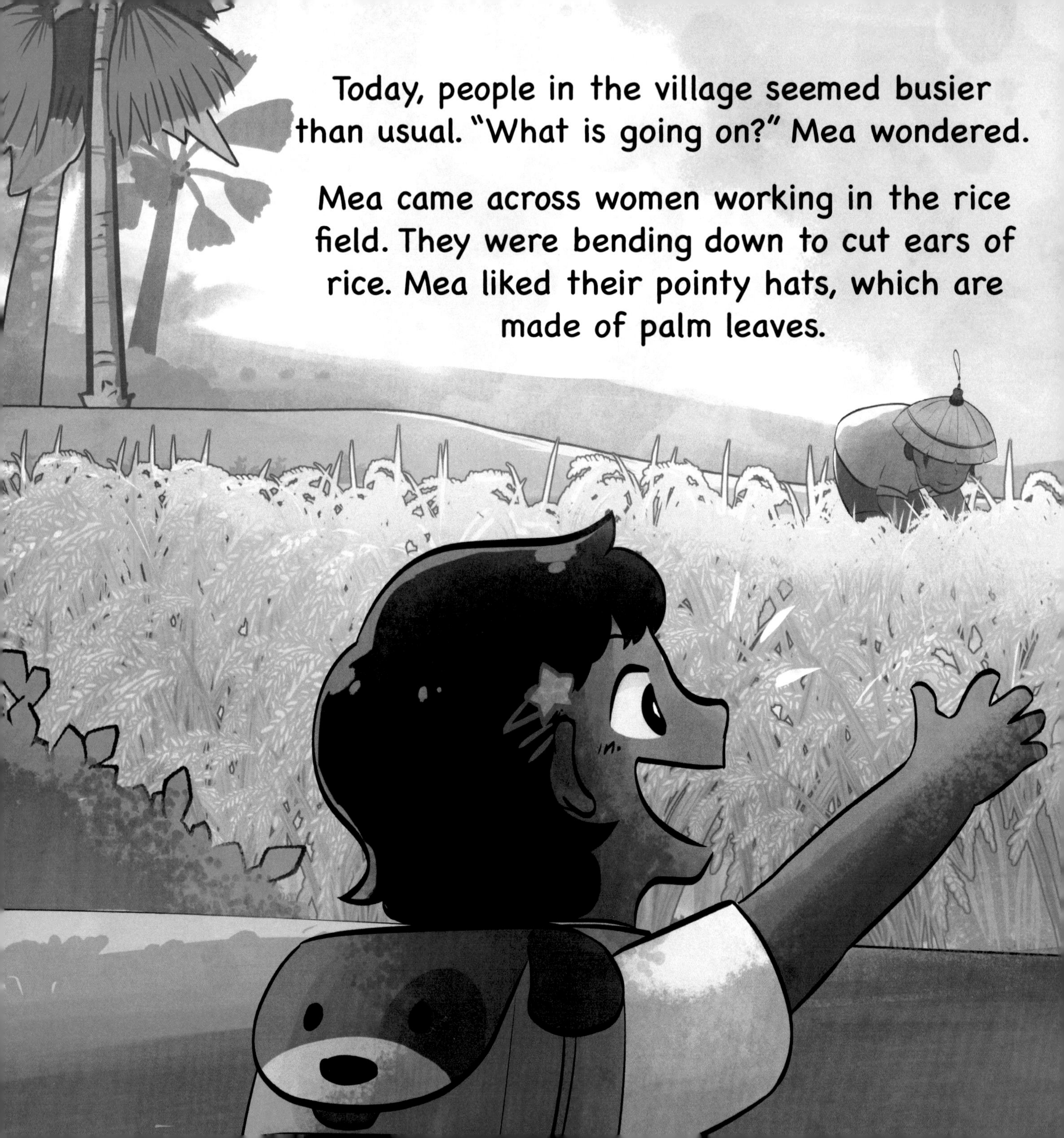

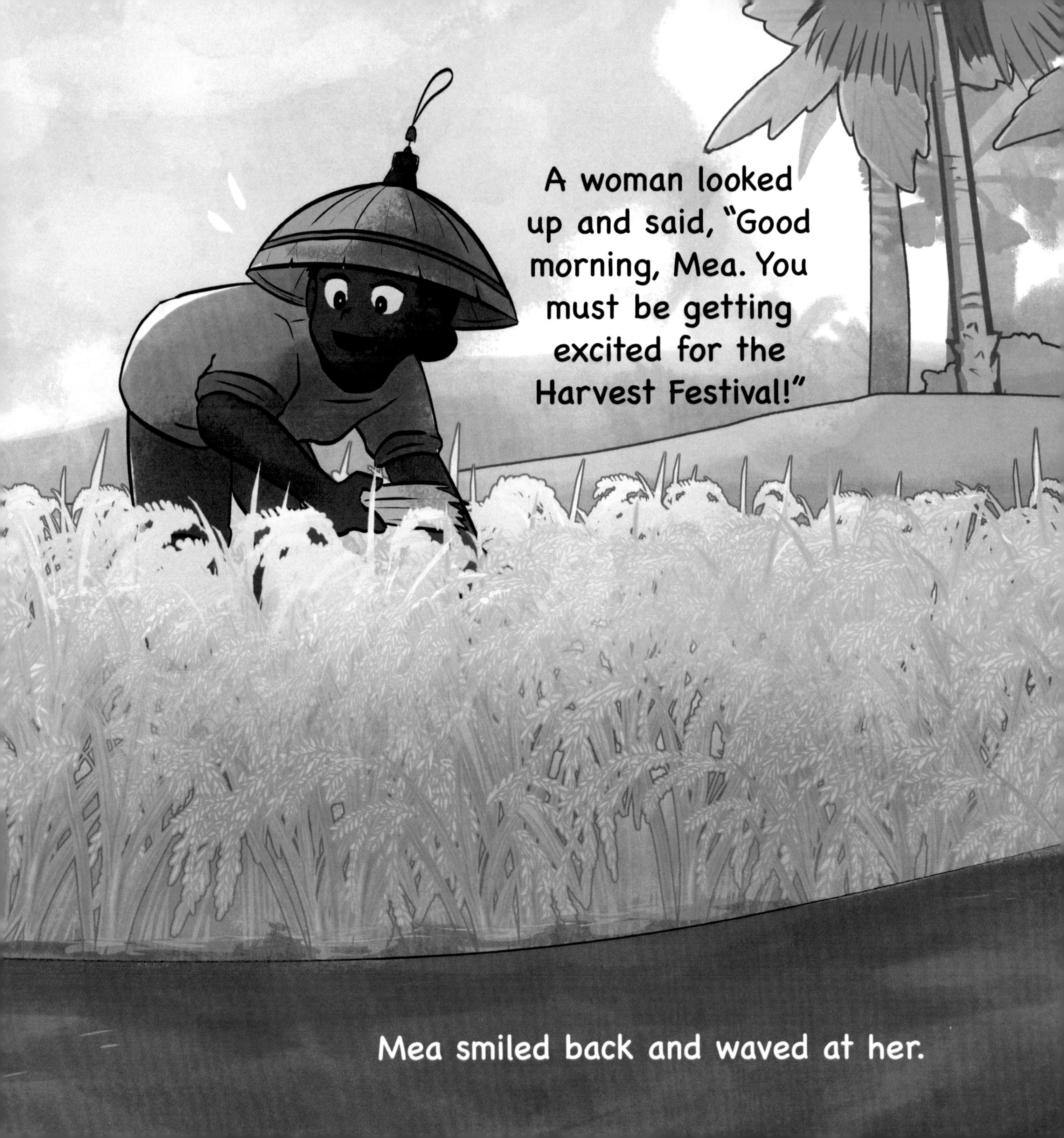

A woman looked up and said, “Good morning, Mea. You must be getting excited for the Harvest Festival!”

Mea smiled back and waved at her.

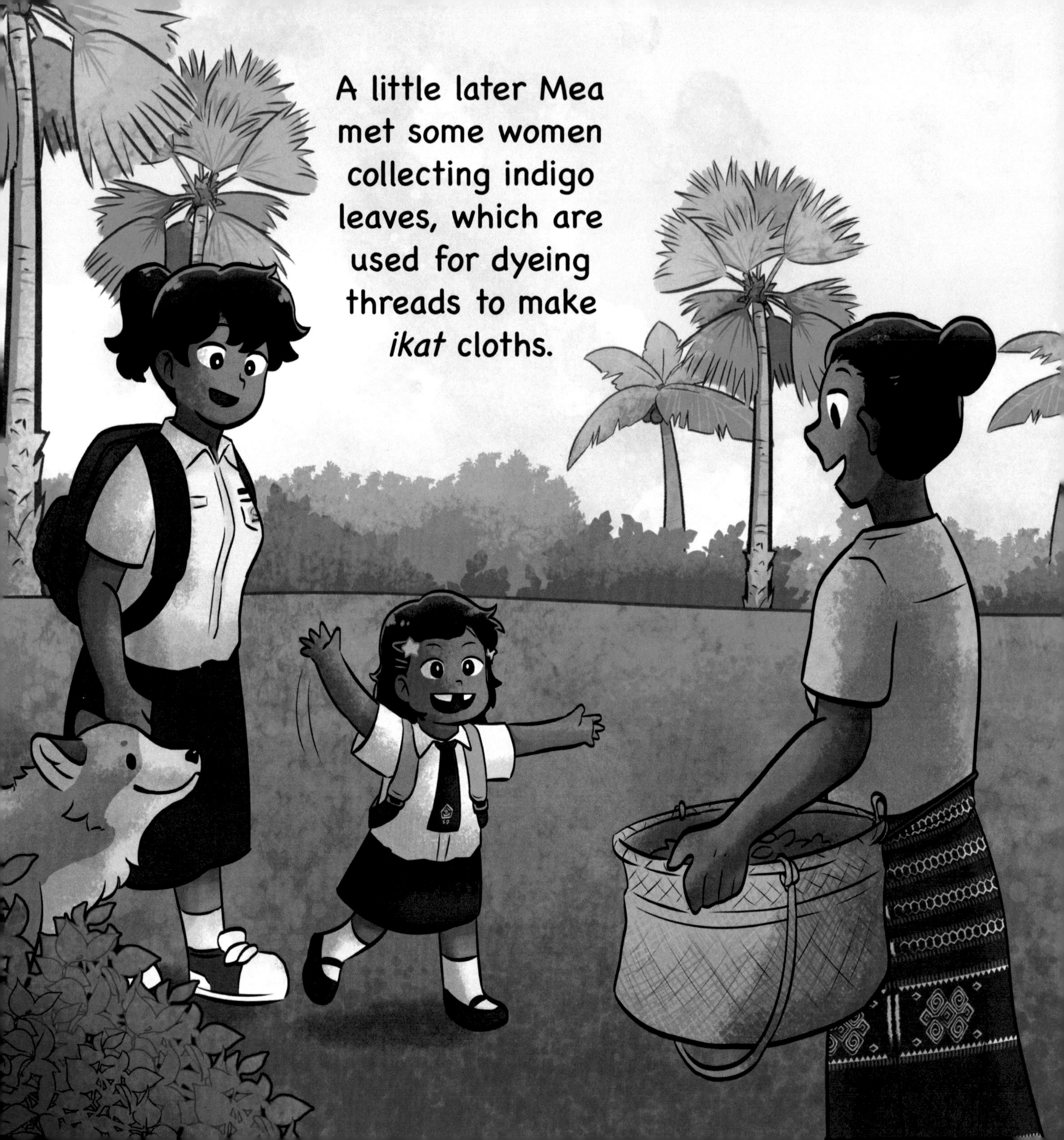

A little later Mea met some women collecting indigo leaves, which are used for dyeing threads to make *ikat* cloths.

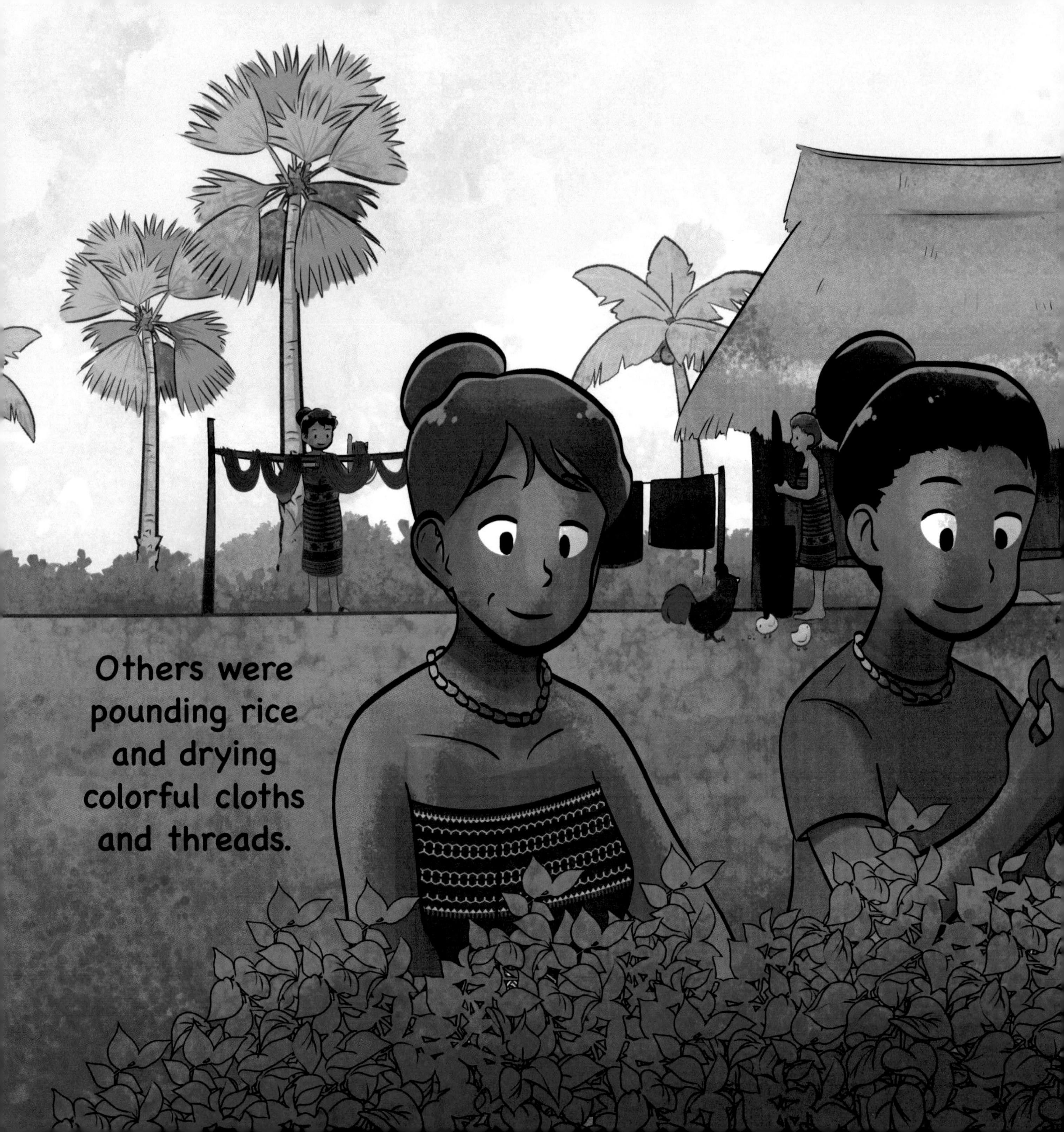

Others were pounding rice and drying colorful cloths and threads.

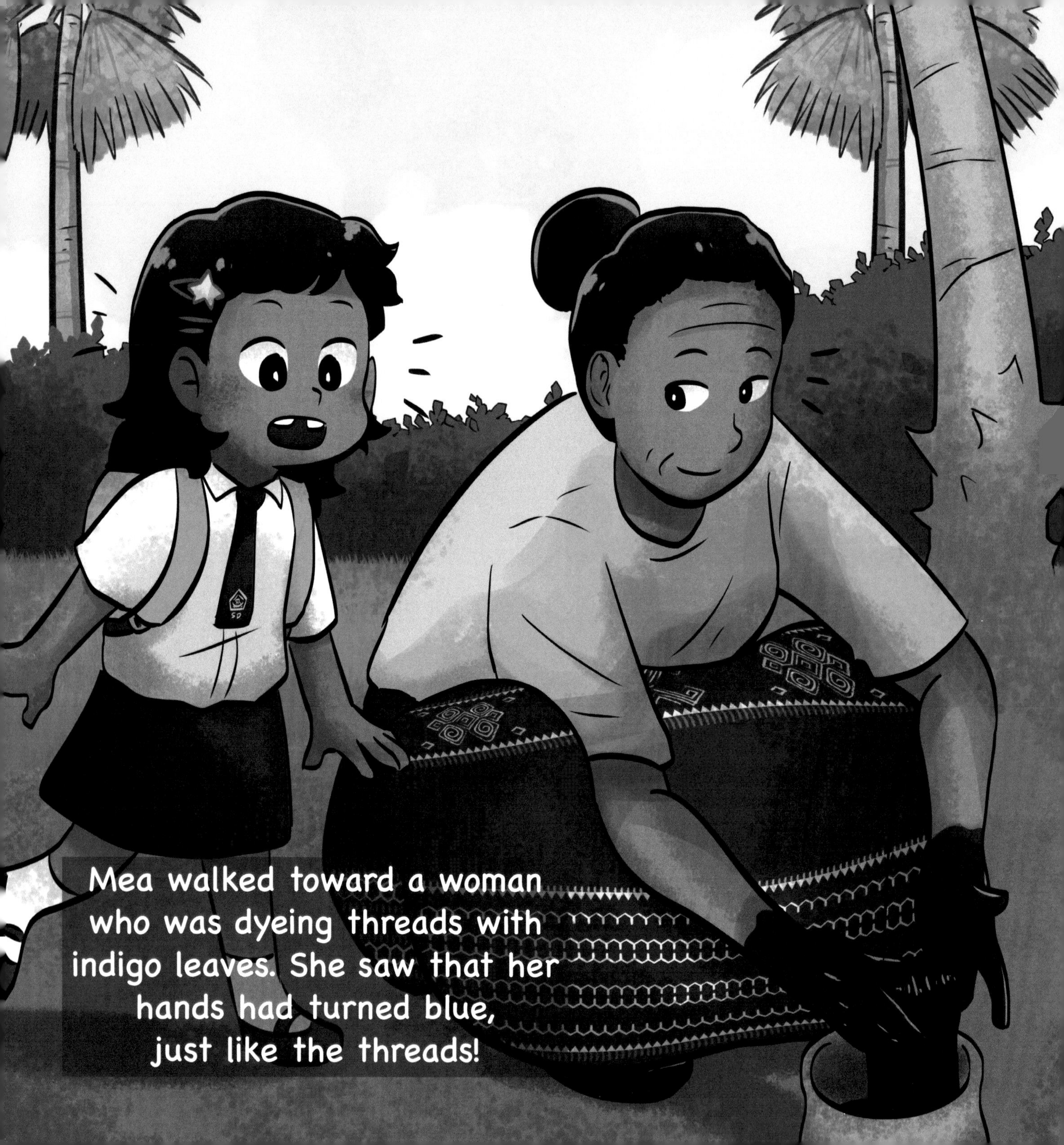
Mea walked toward a woman who was dyeing threads with indigo leaves. She saw that her hands had turned blue, just like the threads!

"Why is everybody working so hard today?" Mea asked.

"Haven't you heard, dear? The Harvest Festival is coming!" the woman replied. "It is time to celebrate, give thanks, and have fun! Everyone in the village will get together. You should be there too, you look old enough to join."

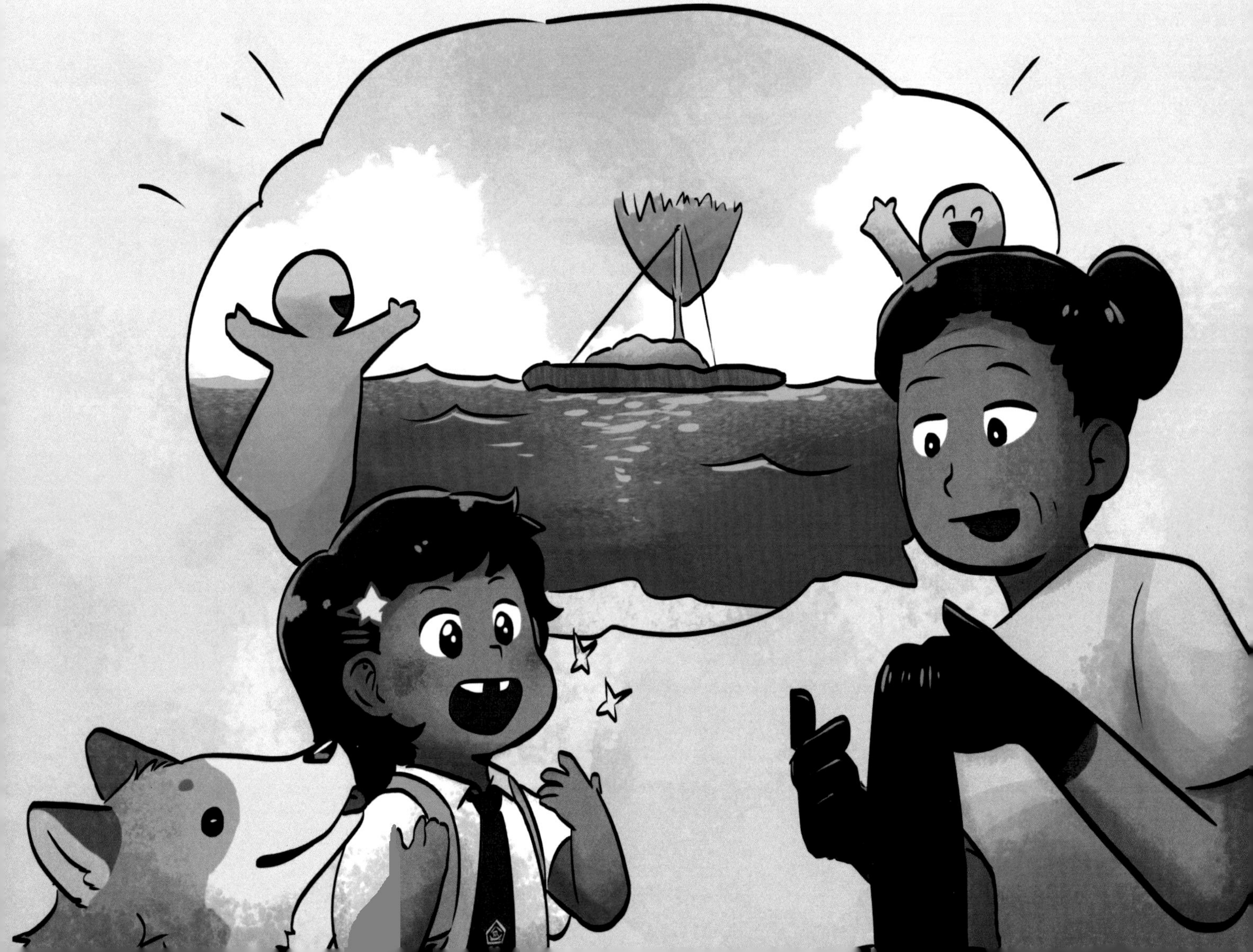

At school, Mea talked excitedly with her friends.

"Do you know that we are going to celebrate the Harvest Festival very soon?"

"This year we are old enough to join the festivities."

"I wonder what it will be like . . .?"

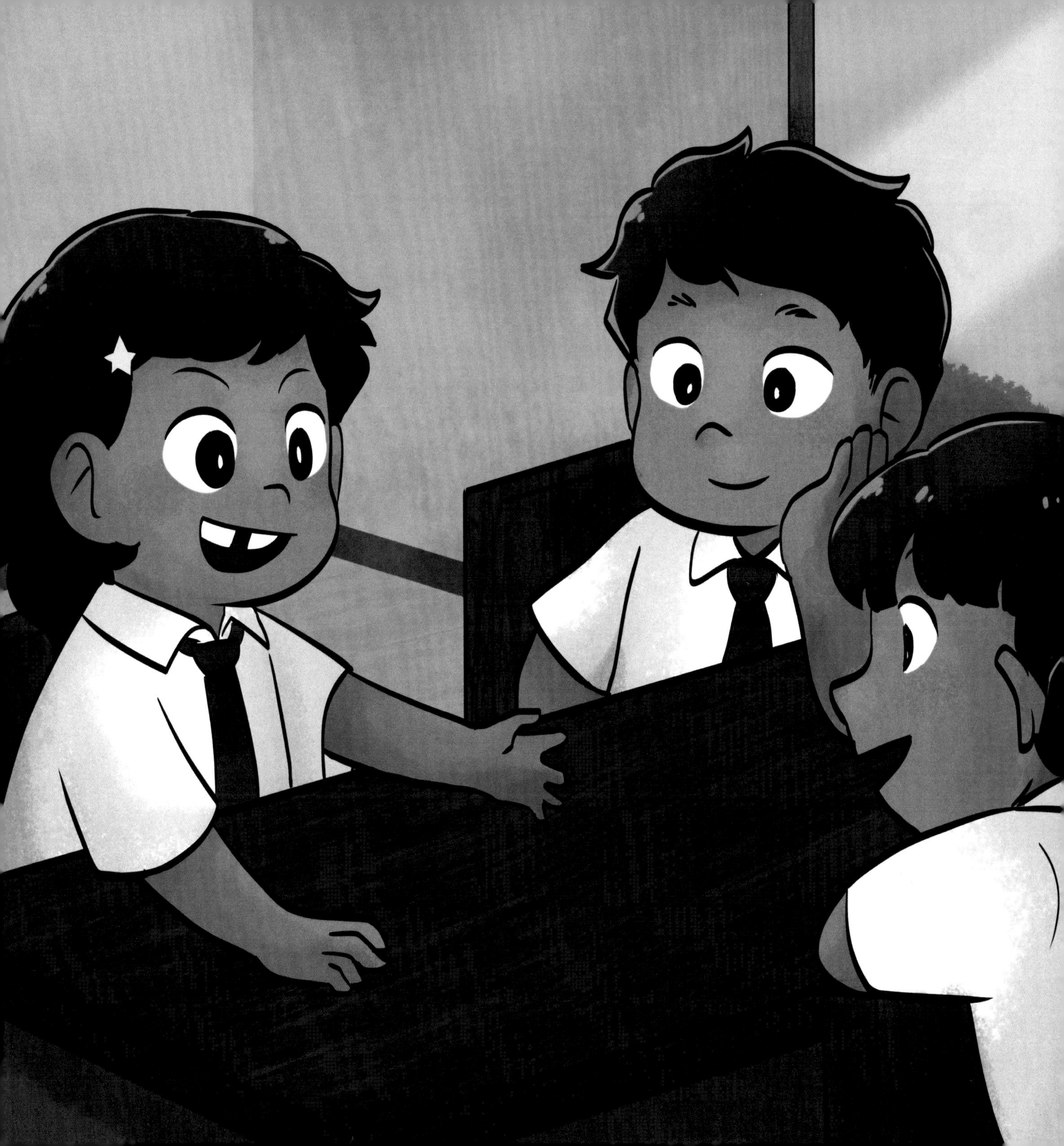

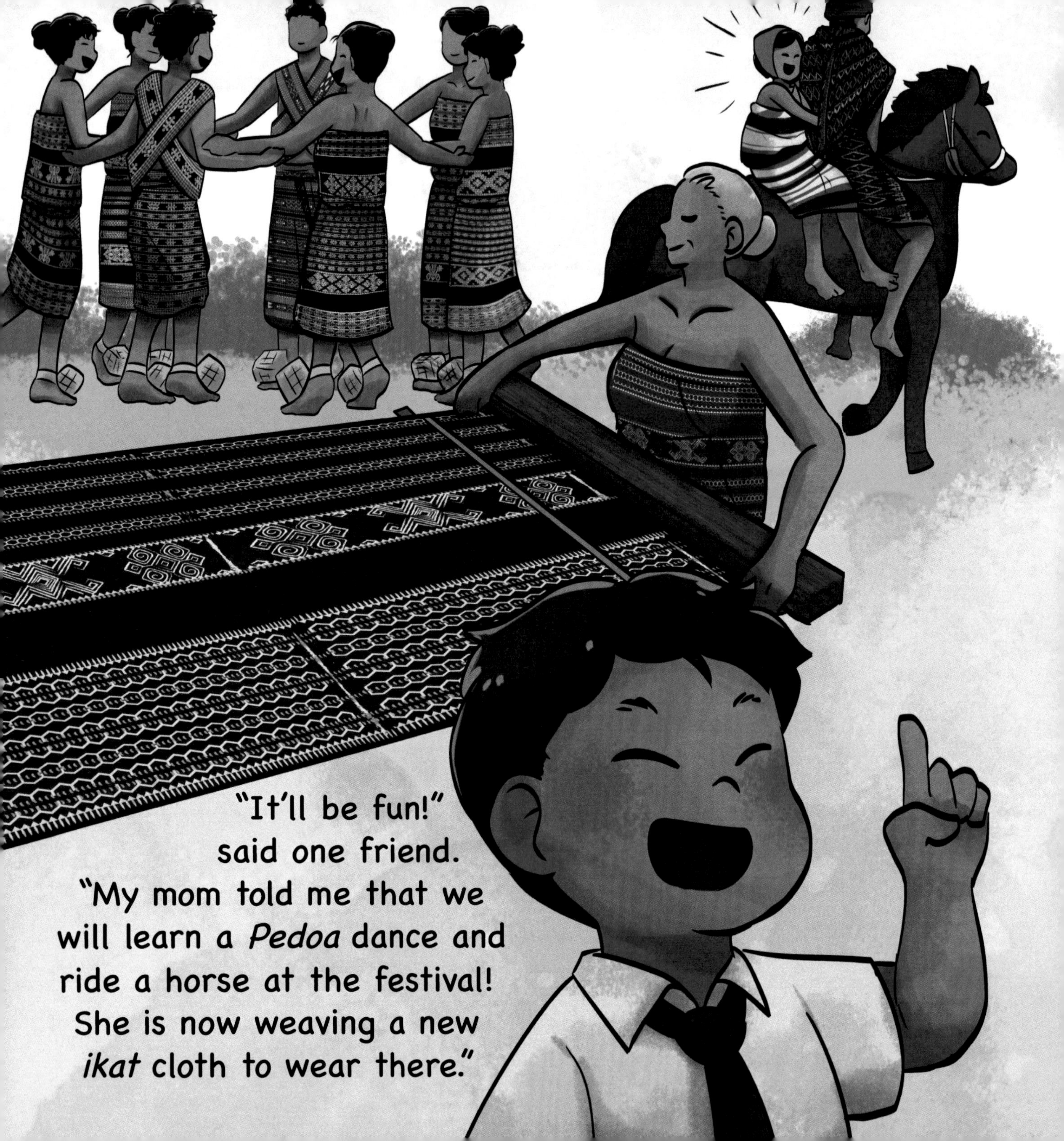

"It'll be fun!" said one friend. "My mom told me that we will learn a *Pedoa* dance and ride a horse at the festival! She is now weaving a new *ikat* cloth to wear there."

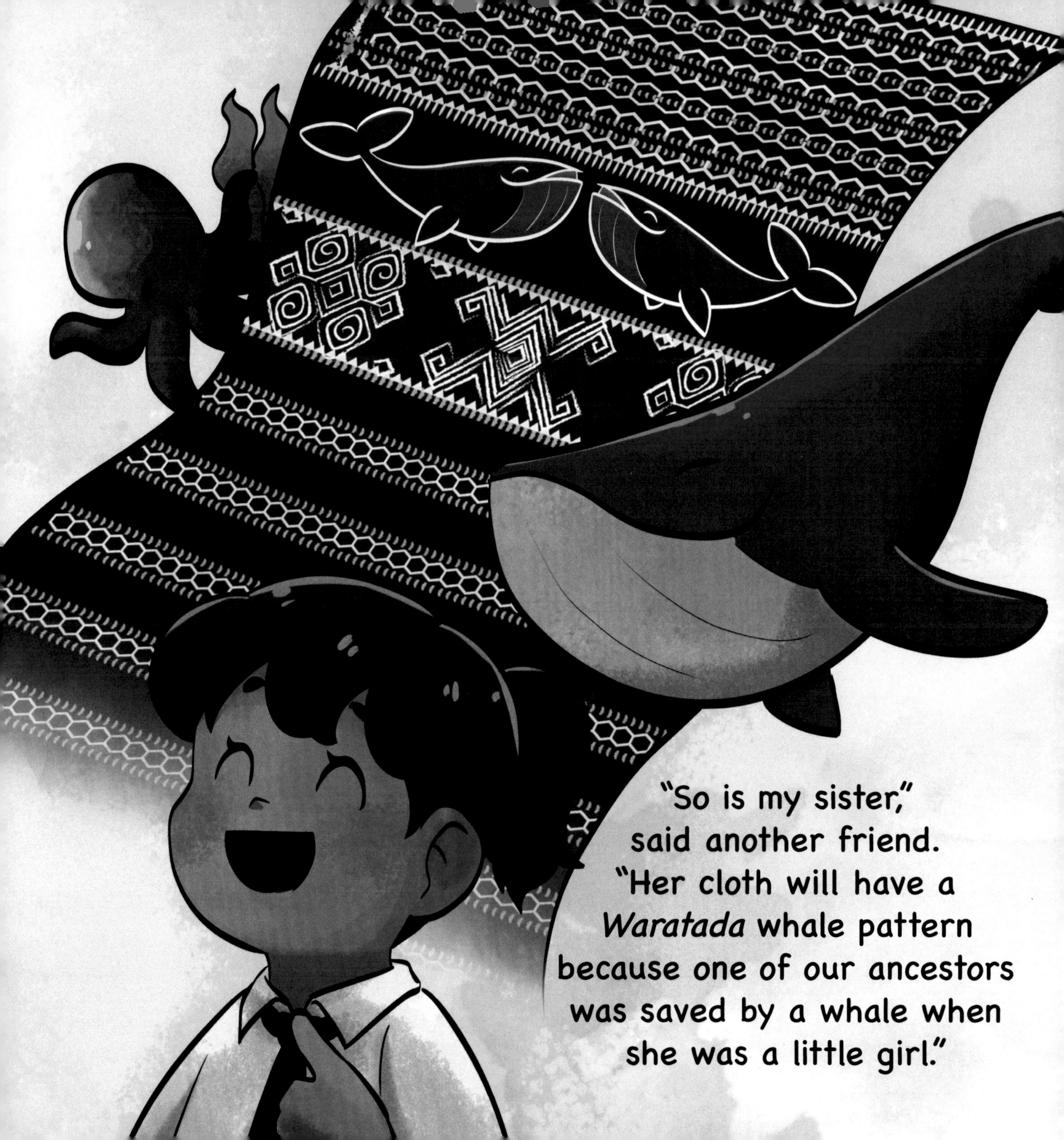

"So is my sister," said another friend. "Her cloth will have a *Waratada* whale pattern because one of our ancestors was saved by a whale when she was a little girl."

"My mom has a pattern called *Wue Jara*," said the third friend, eagerly sharing her family story.

"*Wue Jara* means 'riding on horseback' because one of our ancestors arrived at her wedding on a horse. This pattern always reminds us of her."

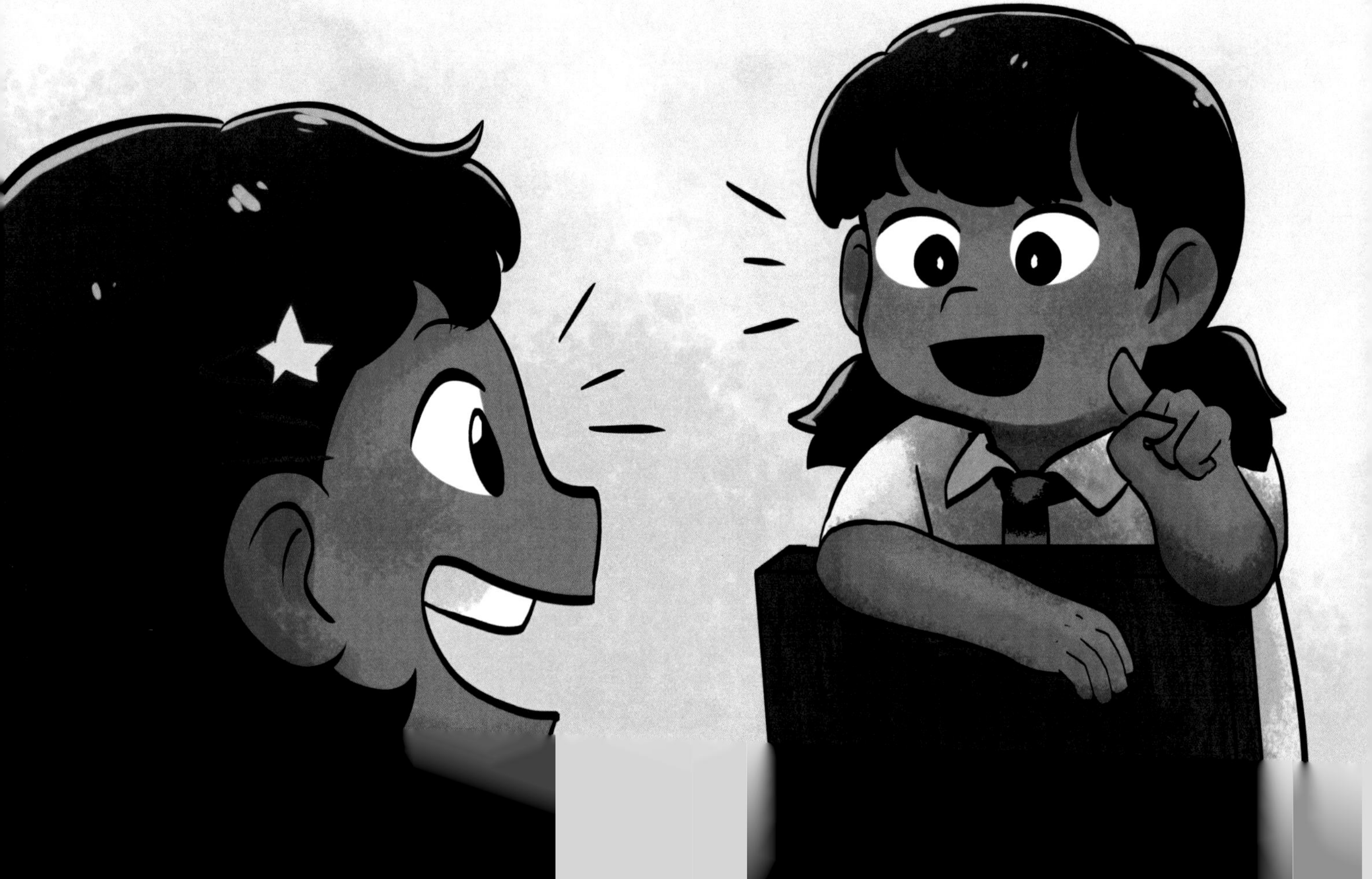

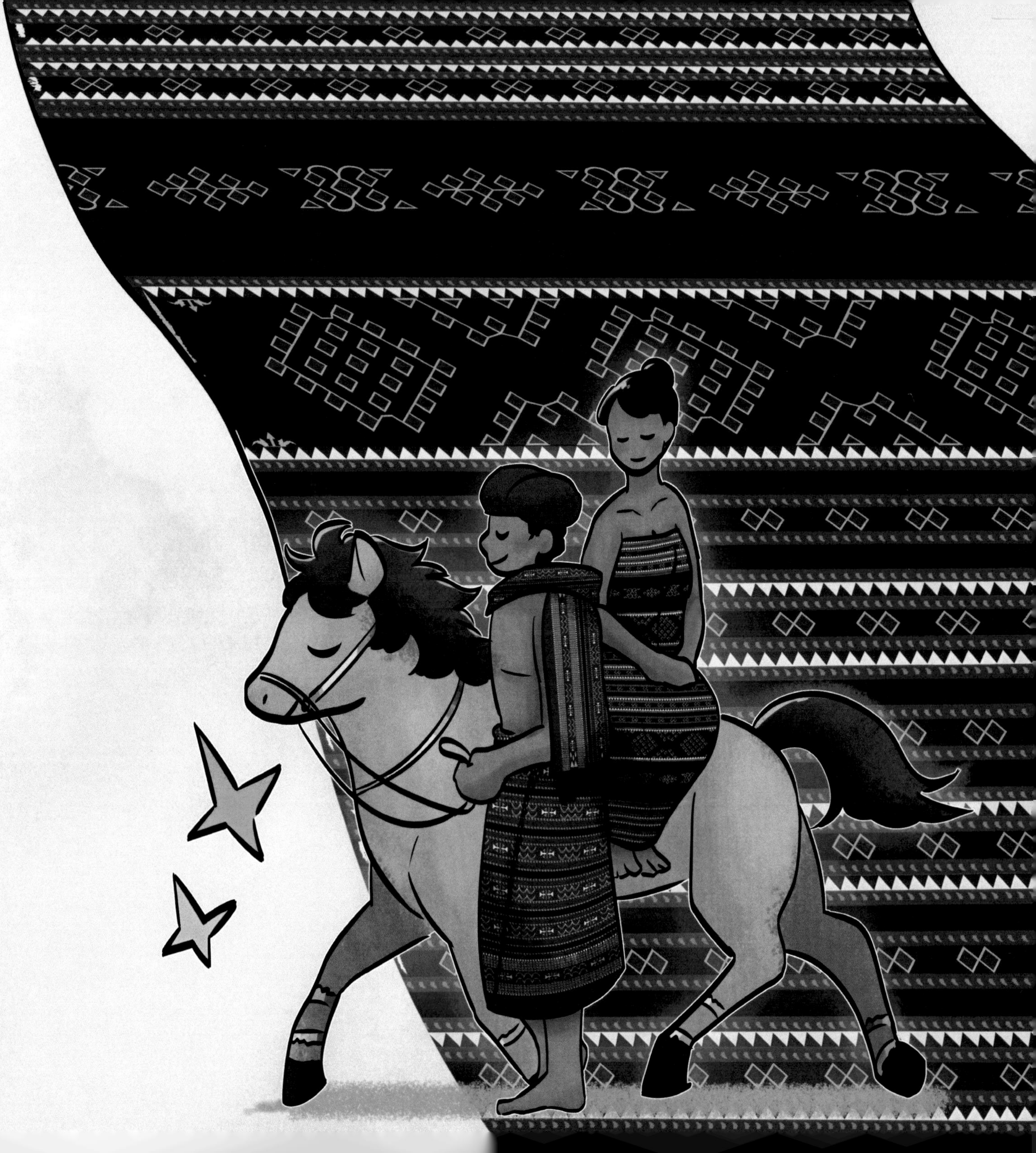

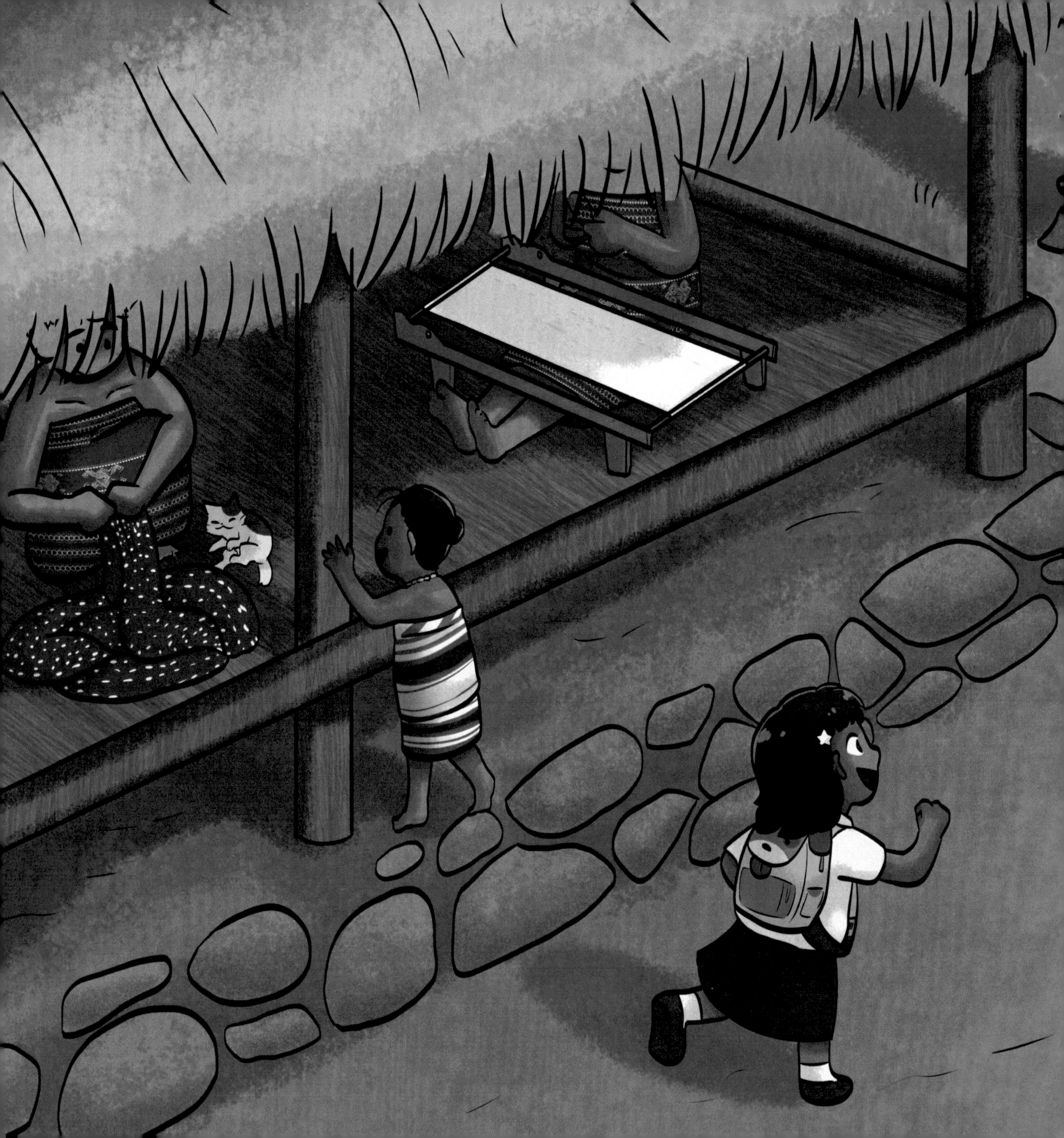

Going home from school, Mea stopped to watch two *ikat* makers working on their front porch.

One woman was tying bundles of threads on the *ikat* frame to make the pattern. The other was cutting off the ties that bound the threads together. when they are dyed.

"I will ask Grandmother to make me an *ikat* cloth too," Mea thought, running as fast as she could to her grandmother's house.

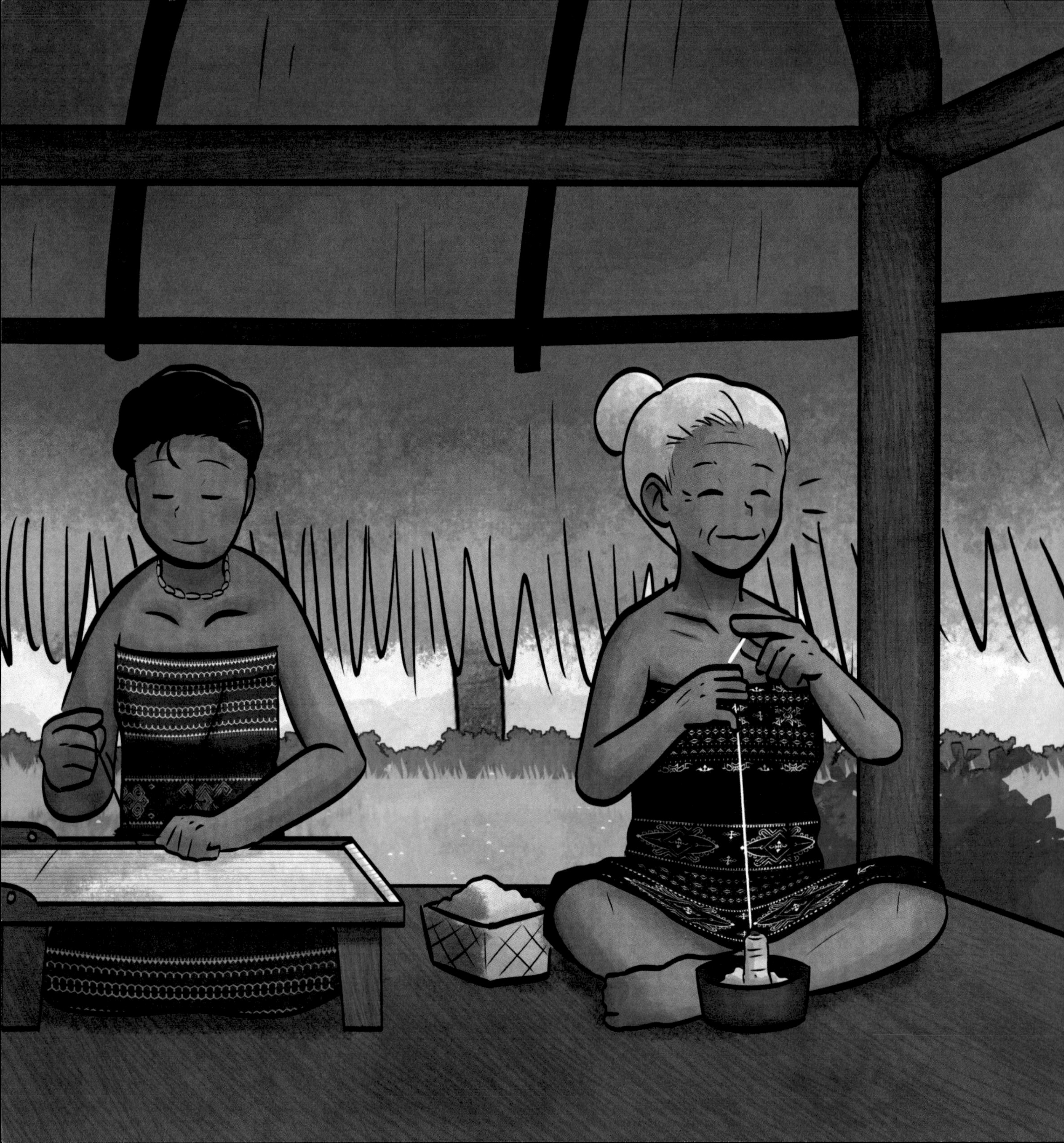

Mea found Grandmother and Mother working on the porch. Mother was tying *ikat* patterns on a frame, while Grandmother was spinning lumps of cotton fibers into thread.

Mea loved watching the fluffs of fiber twist tighter and tighter between Grandmother's fingers.

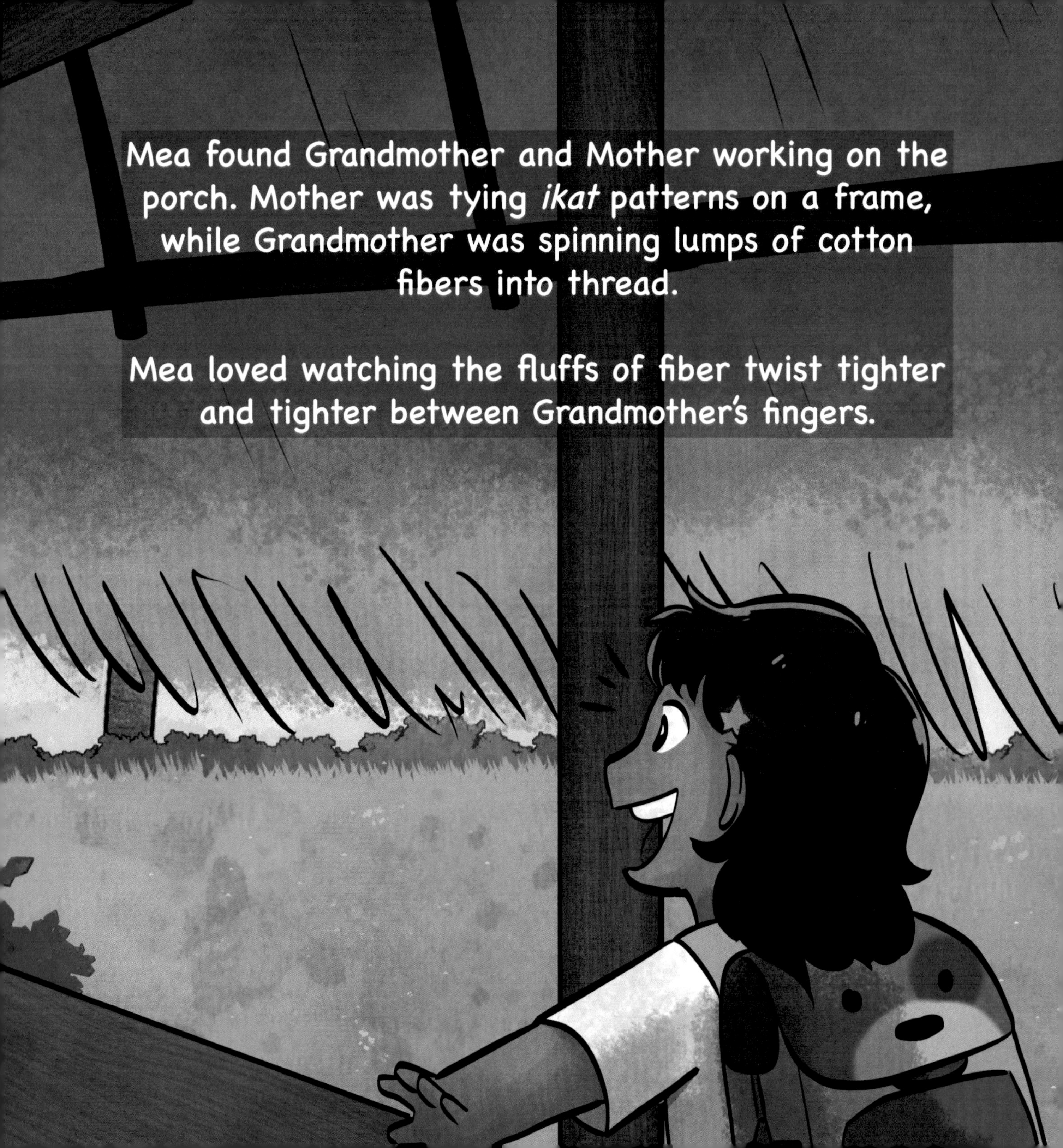

"Granny Epu Beni, can you make me a new *ikat* cloth for the Harvest Festival? I would love to have the *Waratada* whale and *Wue Jara* patterns in my *ikat*, just like my friends."

"Oh, Mea . . ." Grandmother smiled, "We don't make those patterns. They belong to other families."

"But then . . . what patterns do we have?" Mea asked disappointedly.

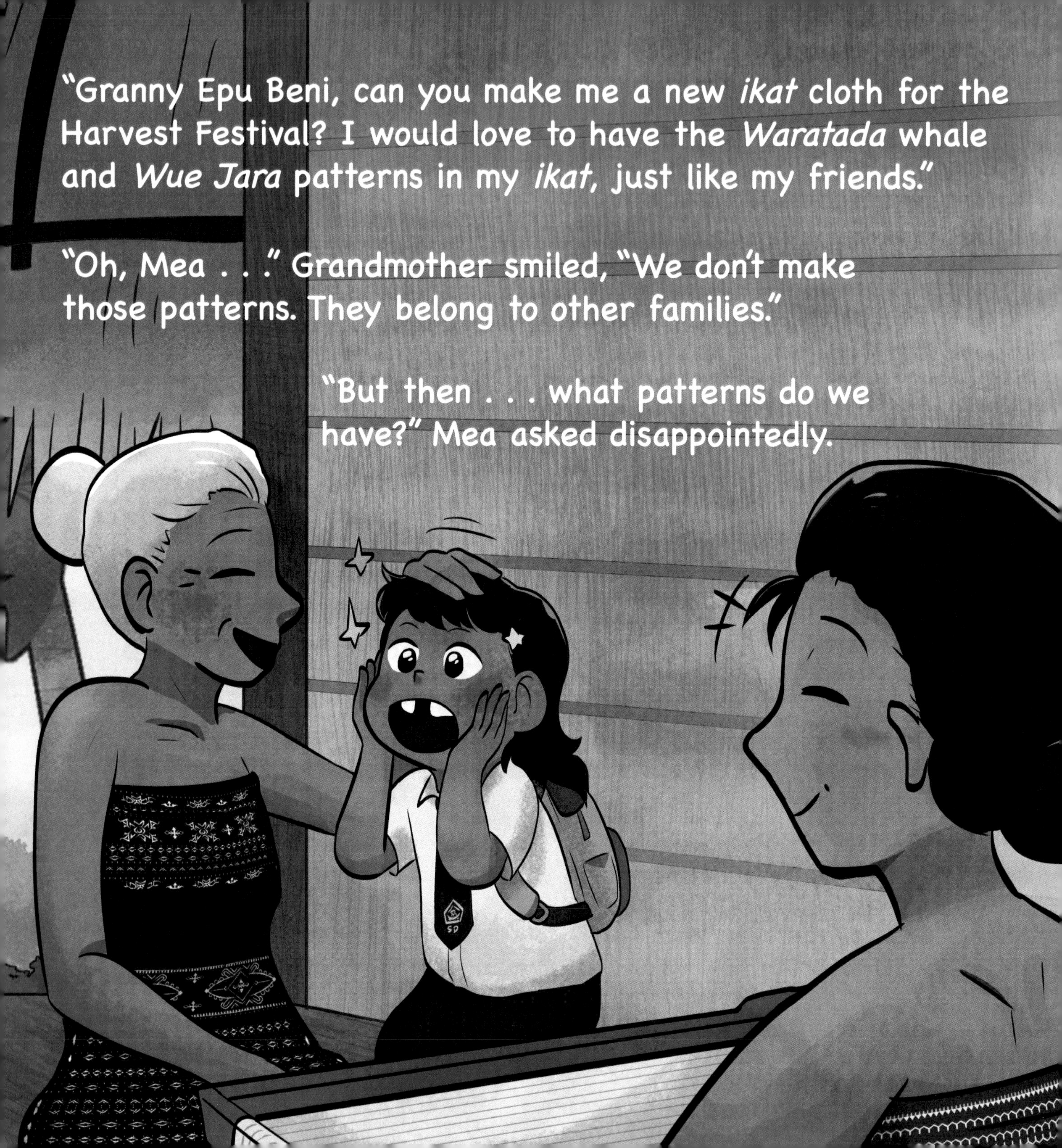

"Well, we have our family's very own special patterns," Mother smiled proudly. "My favorite is the *Patola* pattern."

"Long long ago, one of our ancestors married a king. He gave her a cloth with a *Patola* pattern. Since then, we have been honored to wear this pattern for generations."

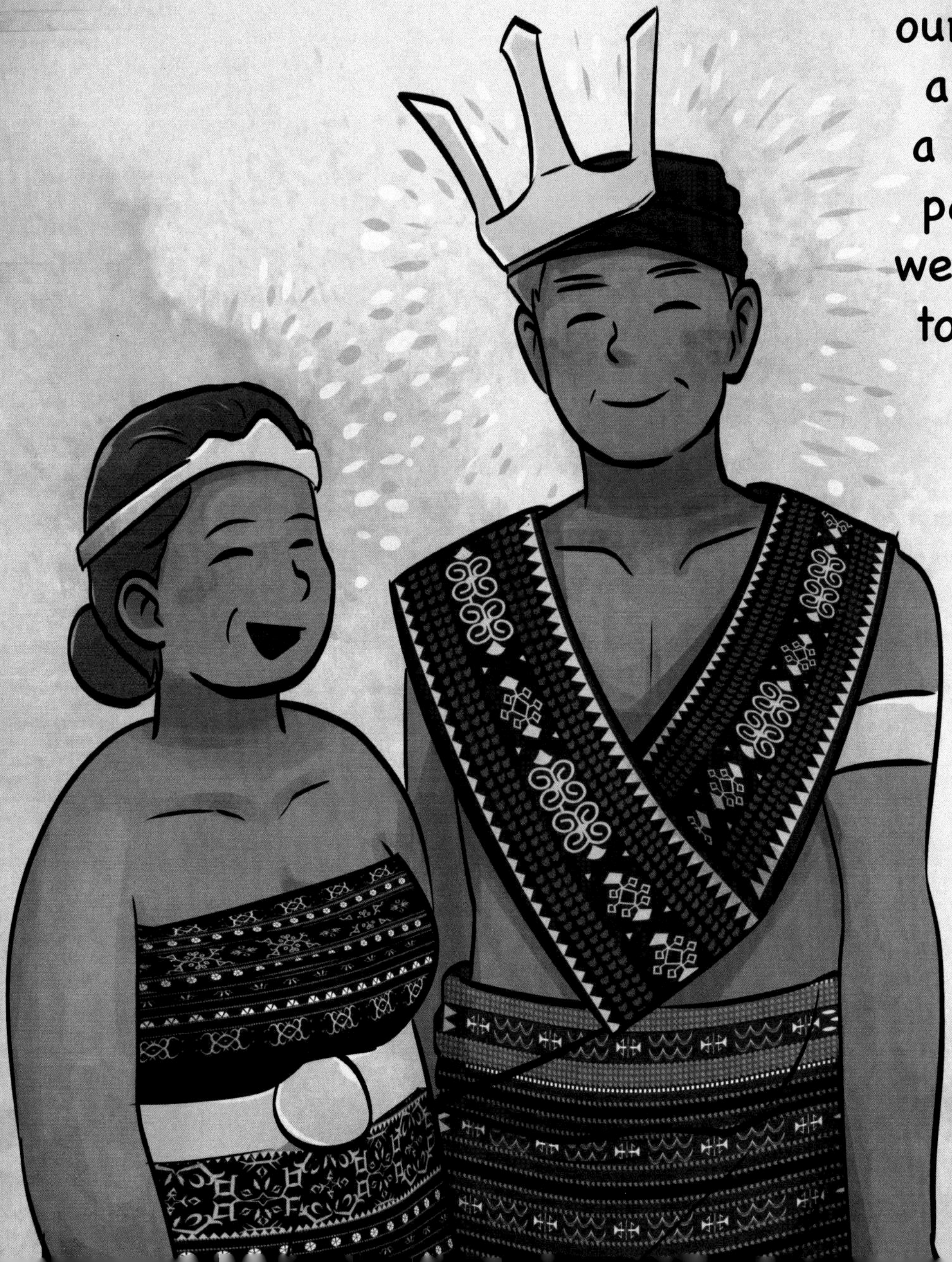

Hearing this story made Mea feel proud of her family pattern.

As each day passed, Mea's excitement about the Harvest Festival grew and grew.

Finally, the first festival day arrived. Mea woke up extra early that morning.

She saw her mother and sister already dressed in their *ikat* sarongs, beautiful tubes of cloth wrapped around their bodies. Both sarongs had the same *Patola* pattern but in different colors.

"Ina, Aa, you look so beautiful!" exclaimed Mea. She could hardly wait for her turn to get dressed in her own sarong.

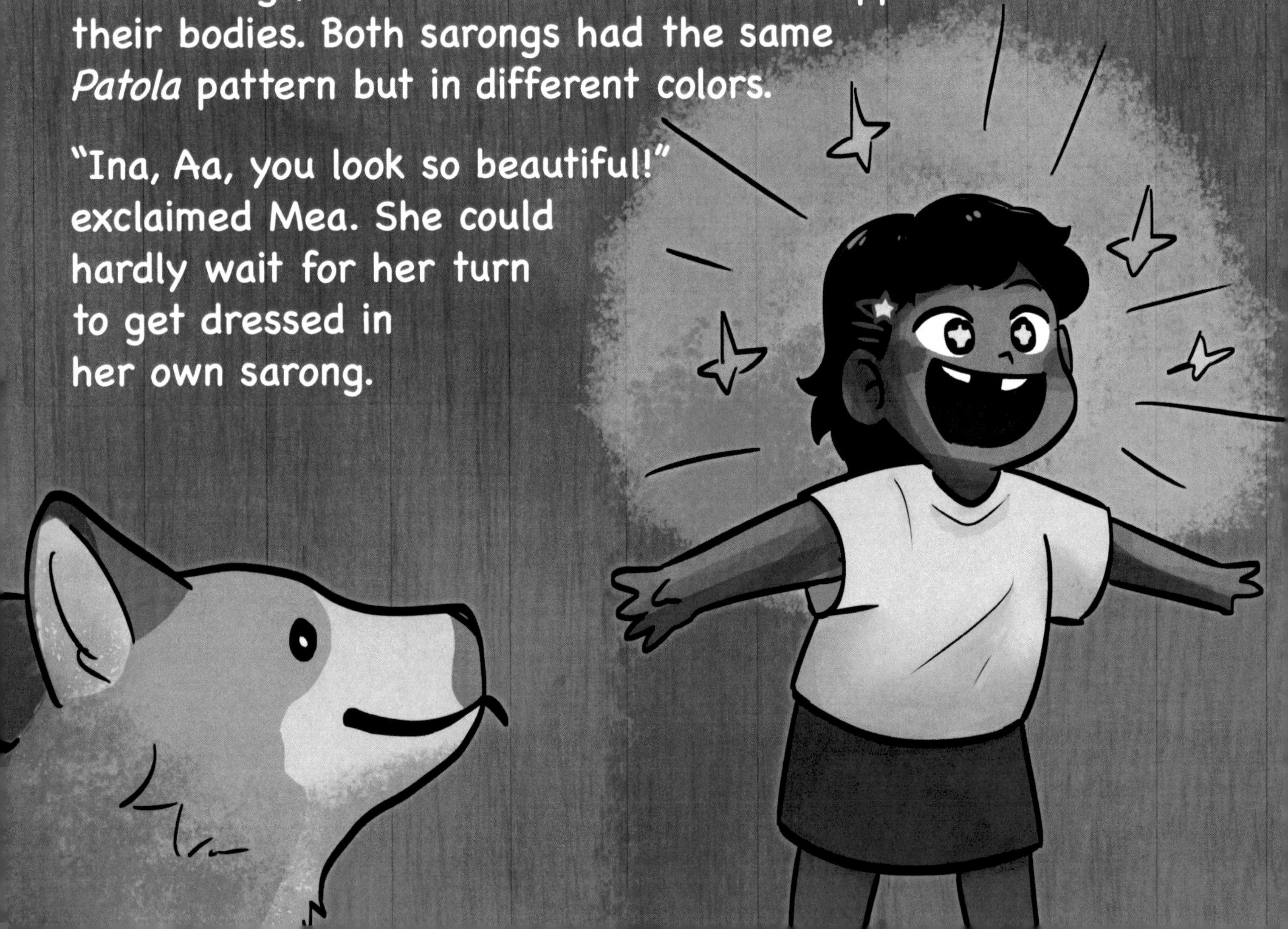

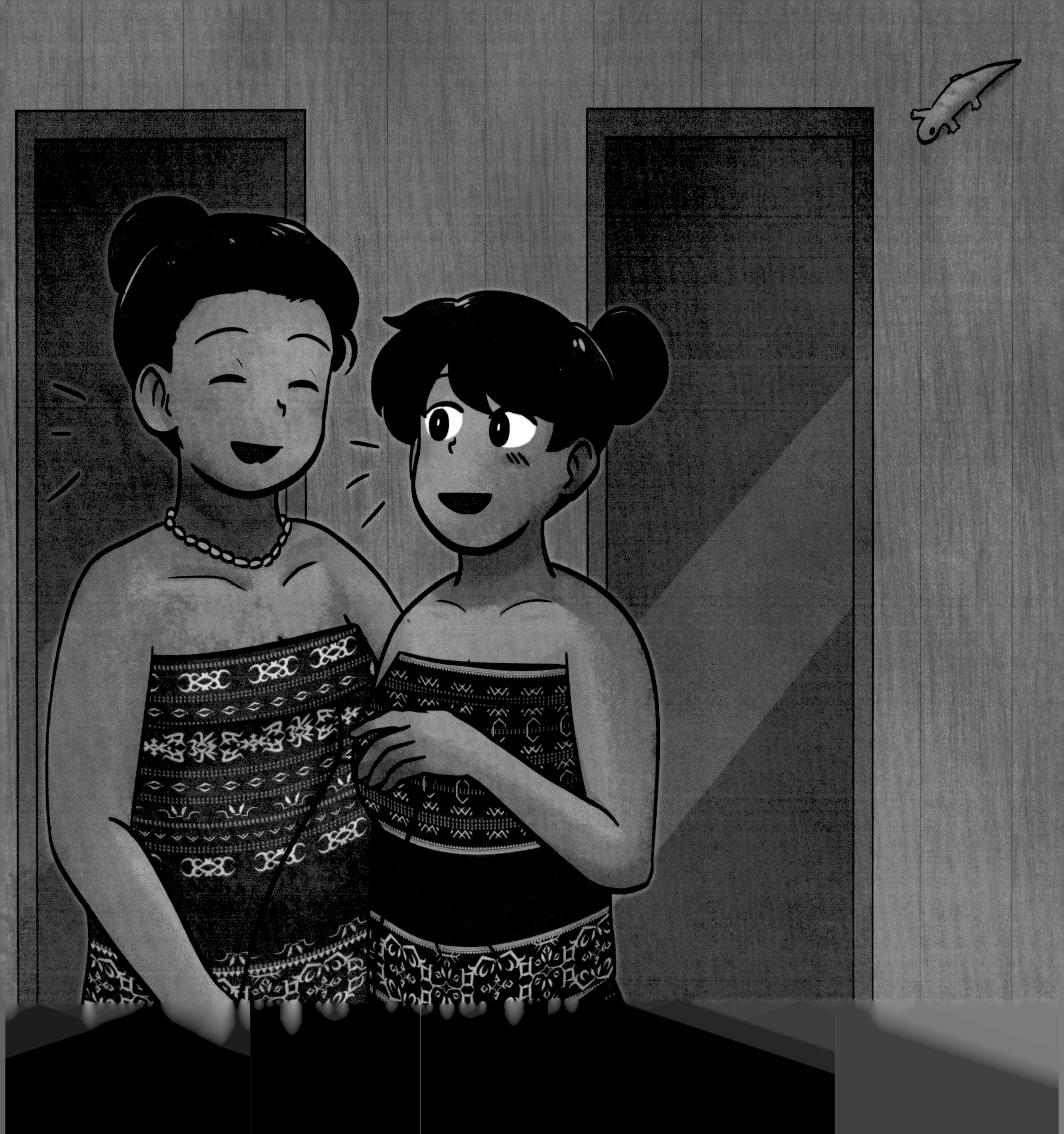

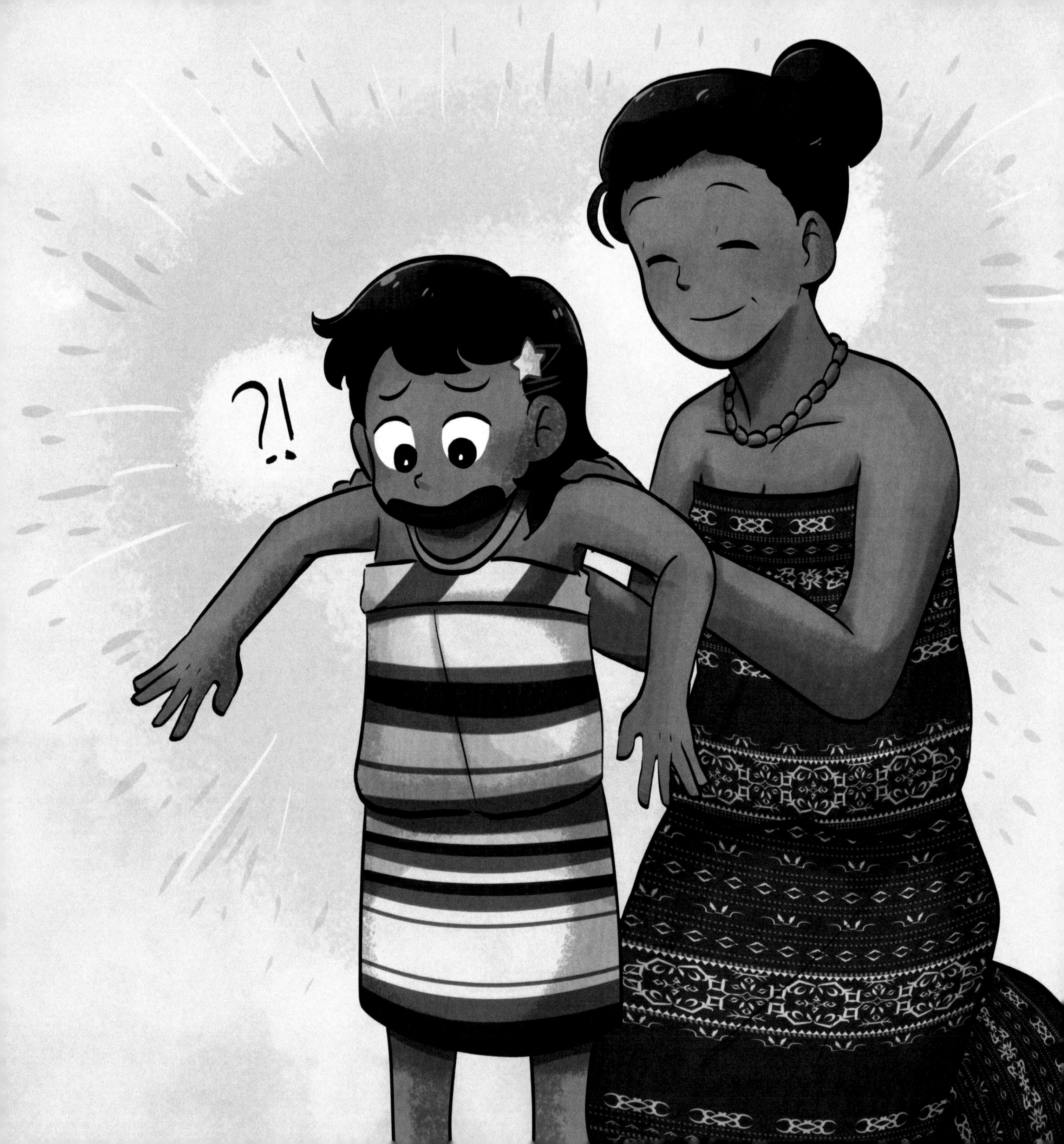
?!

"Come, Mea, let's put on your new sarong," Mother at last called out. "I wove this especially for you."

But when Mea saw her sarong, she frowned.

It didn't look like her mother's or her sister's. There were no *Patola* patterns, there were no patterns at all! Just row after row of stripes!

"Ina, I don't like this sarong. It is not beautiful like yours, it is just stripy and boring!"

"Why do I have to wear this?"

Mother gently stroked Mea's shoulder.

"Your sarong is called *ei leko wue.* It is special for a girl your age. When you are as old as your sister, then you can wear our family patterns."

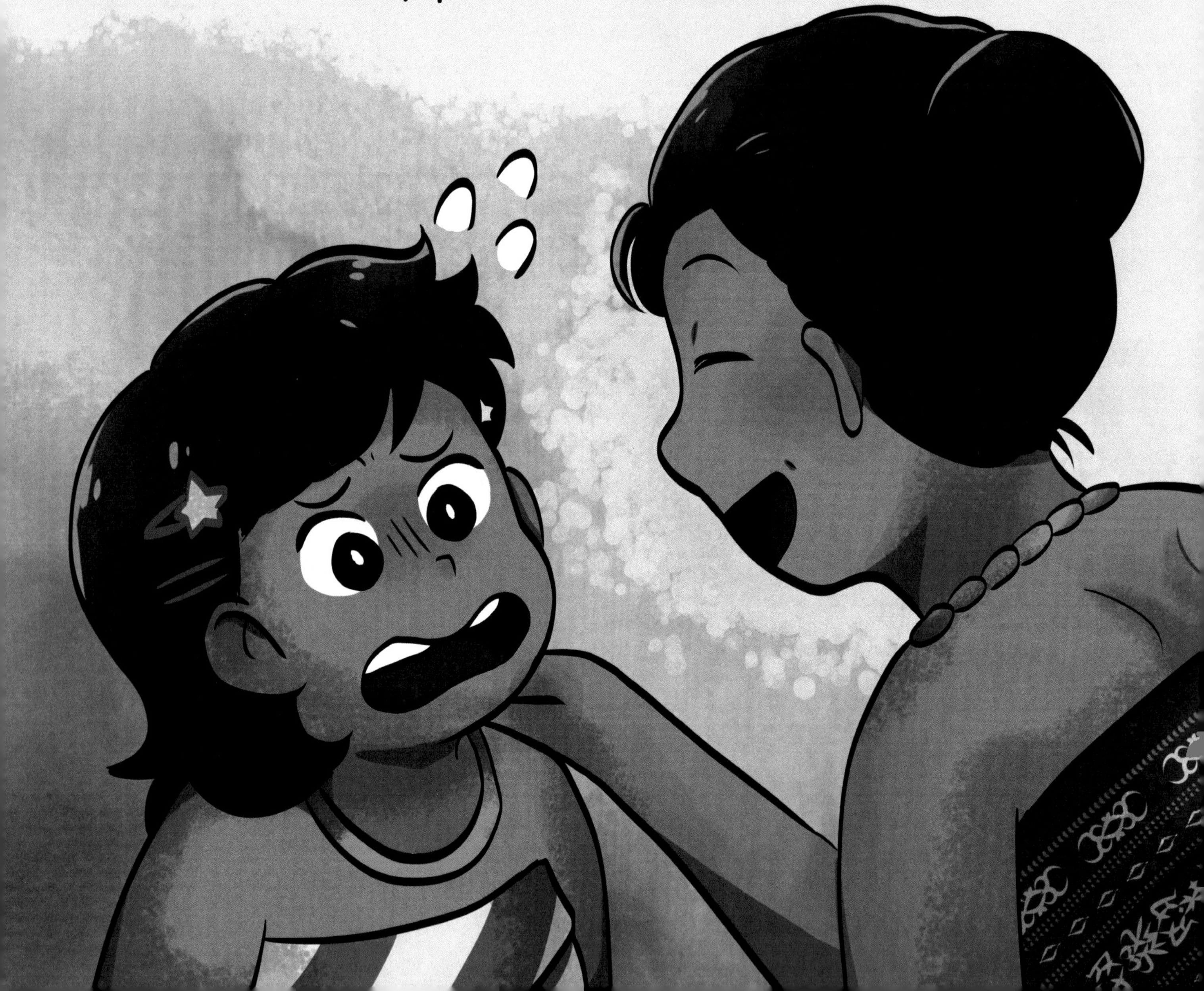

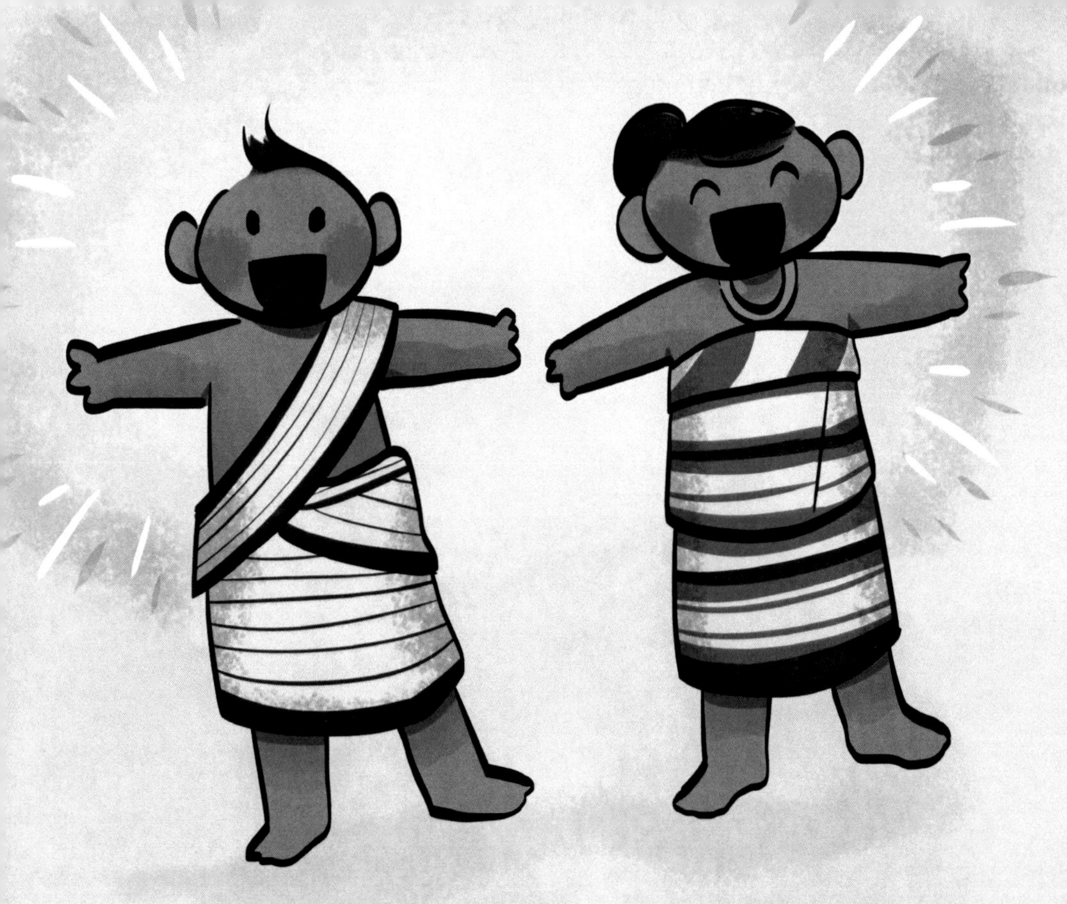

But Mea was not happy with promises about the future.

She wanted it now!

She was very worried that she would be the only person wearing a boring striped sarong at the festival.

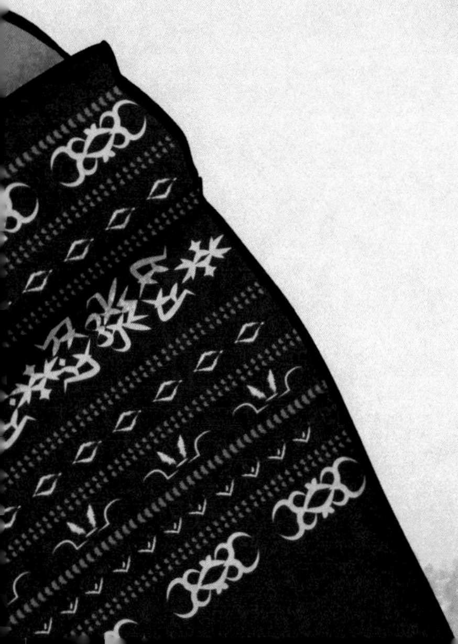

All the way to the festival, Mea imagined that all her friends would be wearing special sarongs with their family patterns, all of them except her!

The closer she got to the festival, the worse she felt.

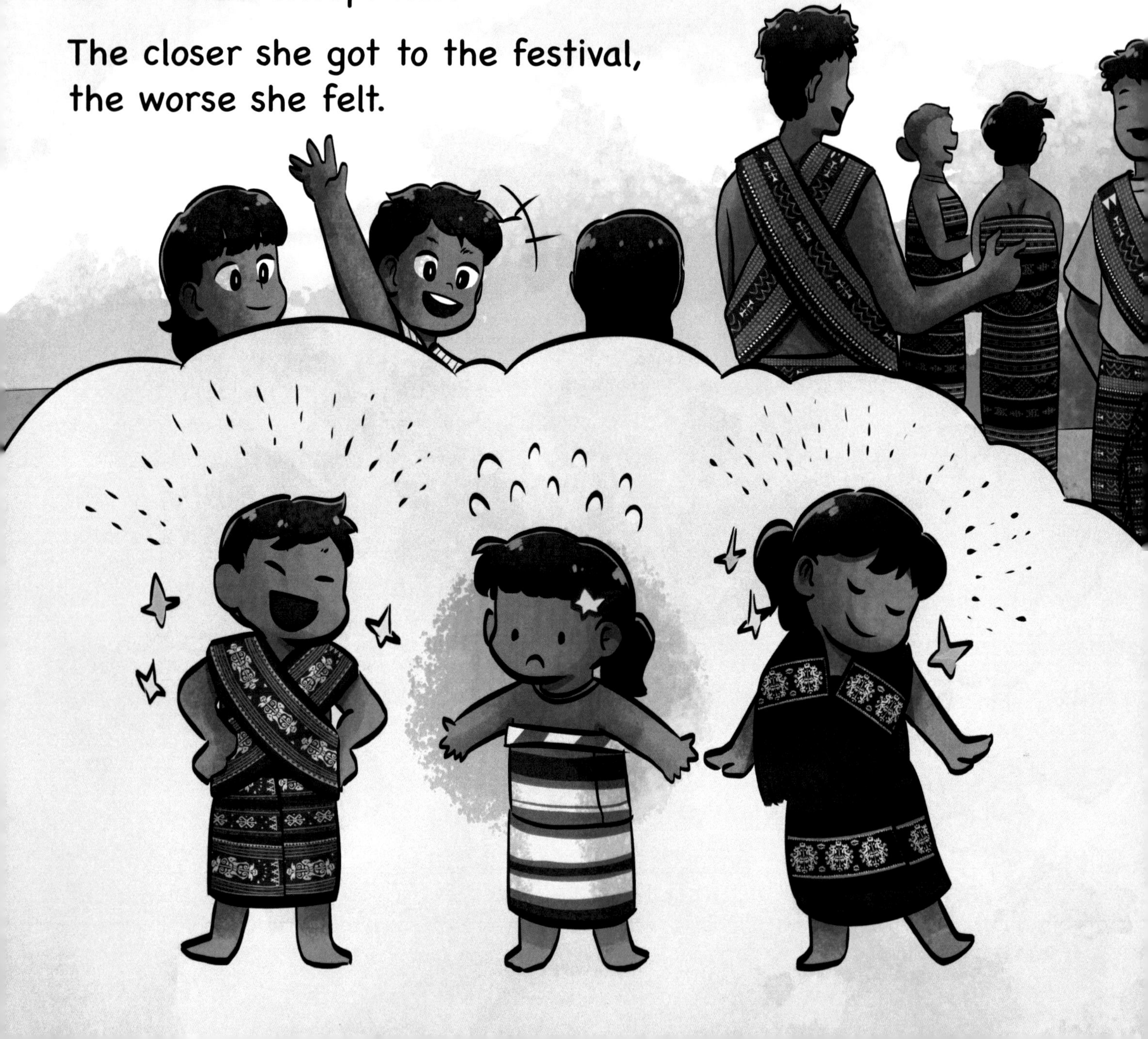

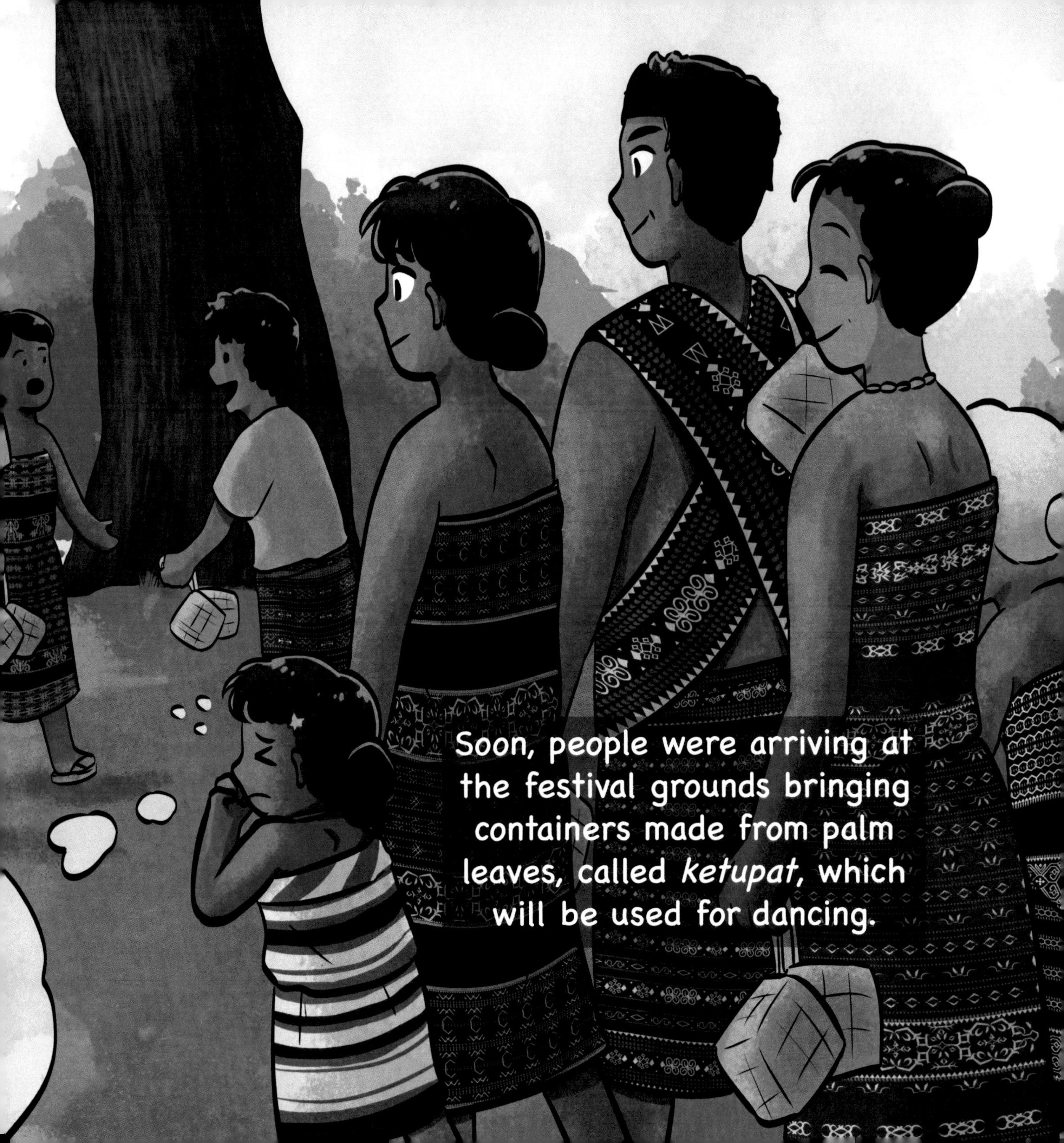

Soon, people were arriving at the festival grounds bringing containers made from palm leaves, called *ketupat*, which will be used for dancing.

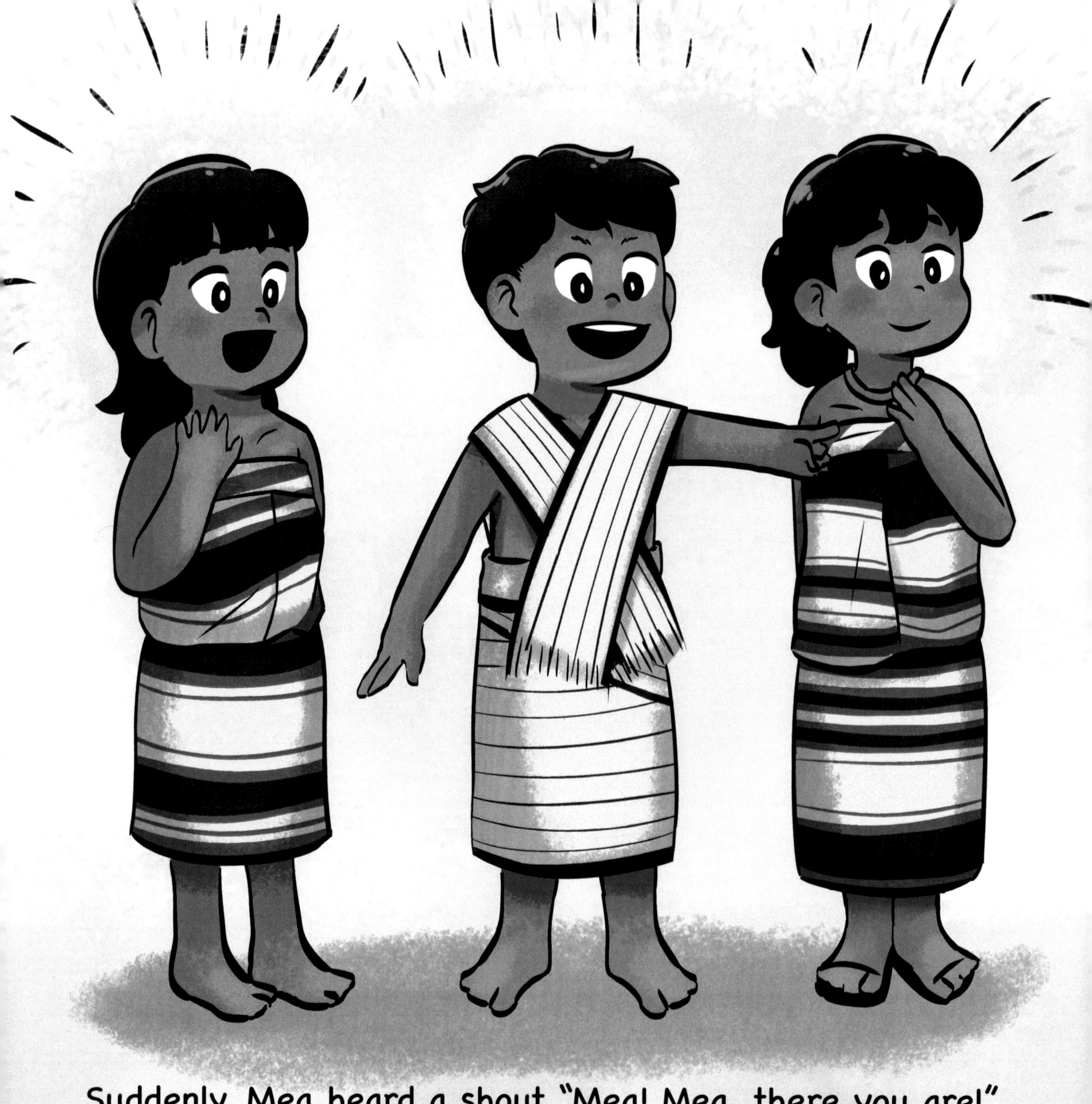

Suddenly, Mea heard a shout. "Mea! Mea, there you are!"

Mea turned and saw her school friends . . . Oh, what a relief! They were all wearing stripes, just like her!

In fact, every little girl was wearing a striped *ei leko wue*, and every little boy was wearing a striped *hi'i leko wue*. There were thick stripes, thin stripes, and all kinds of stripes! Mea didn't feel left out anymore.

Before long, the festival was in full swing. People from villages near and far came to celebrate into the night.

Mea and her friends joined the *Pedoa* dance. They stood in a circle, linking arms with their neighbors.

Mea followed the other dancers, stepping forward and back, humming along with the singing and chanting.

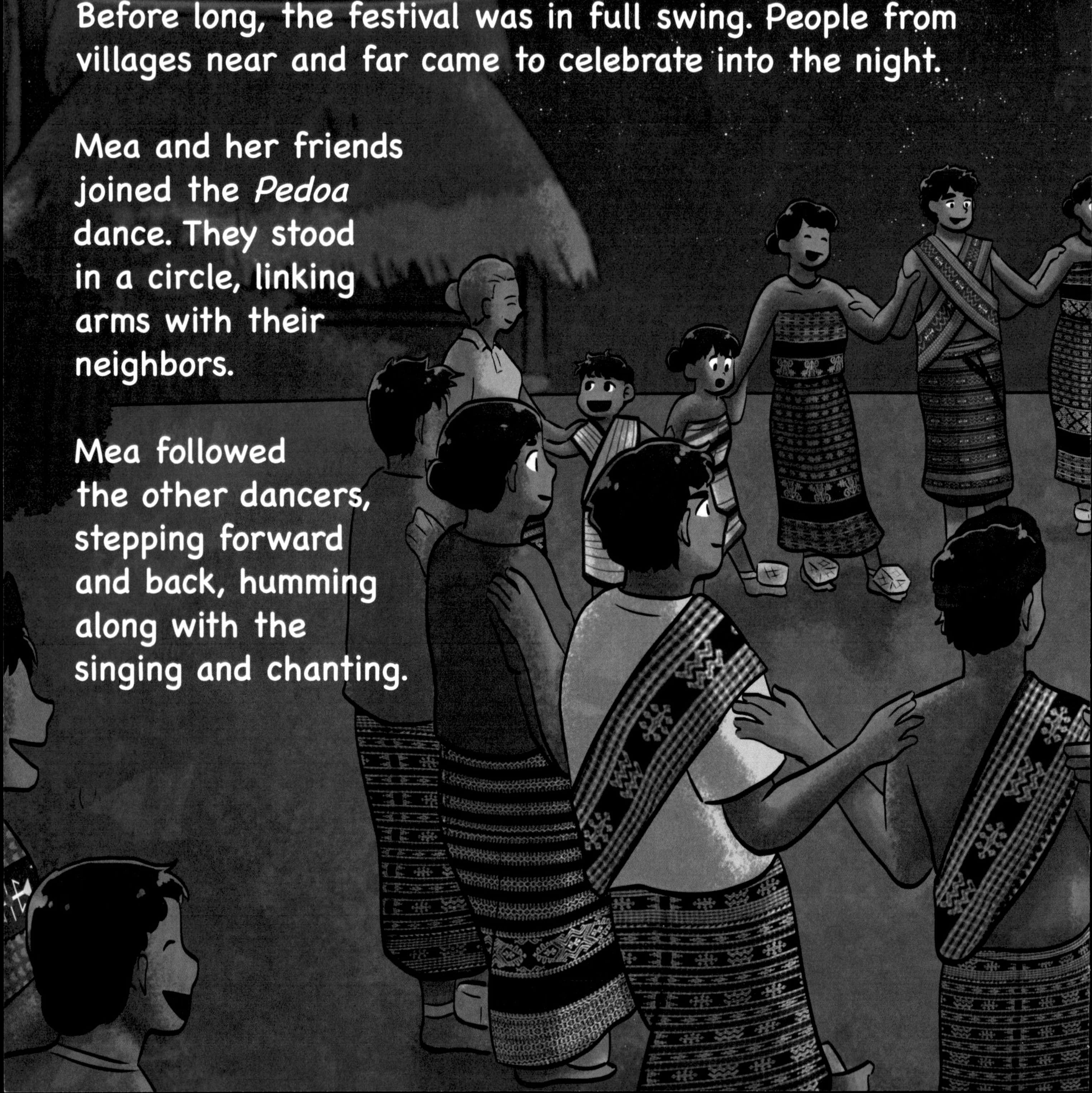

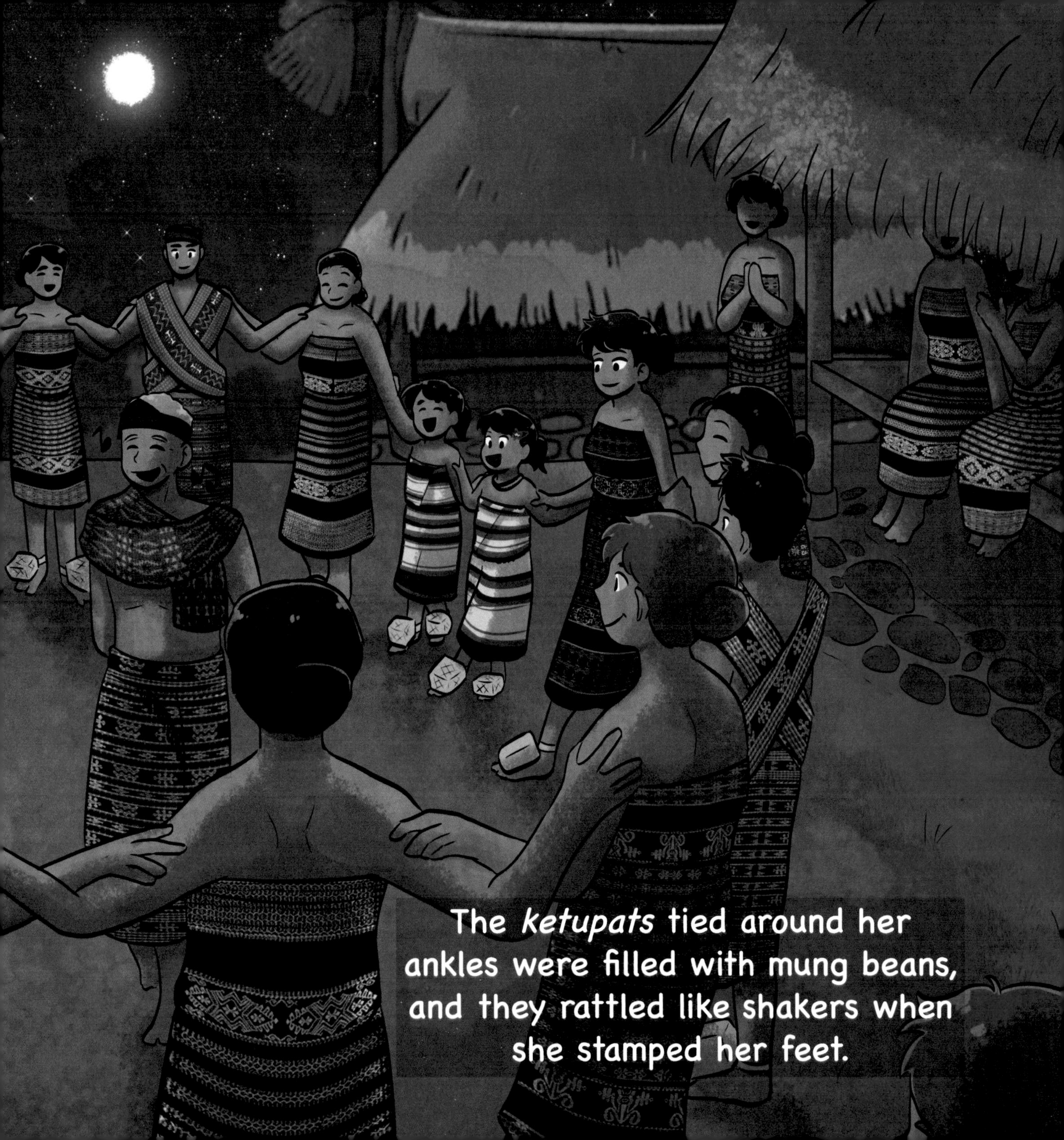

The *ketupats* tied around her ankles were filled with mung beans, and they rattled like shakers when she stamped her feet.

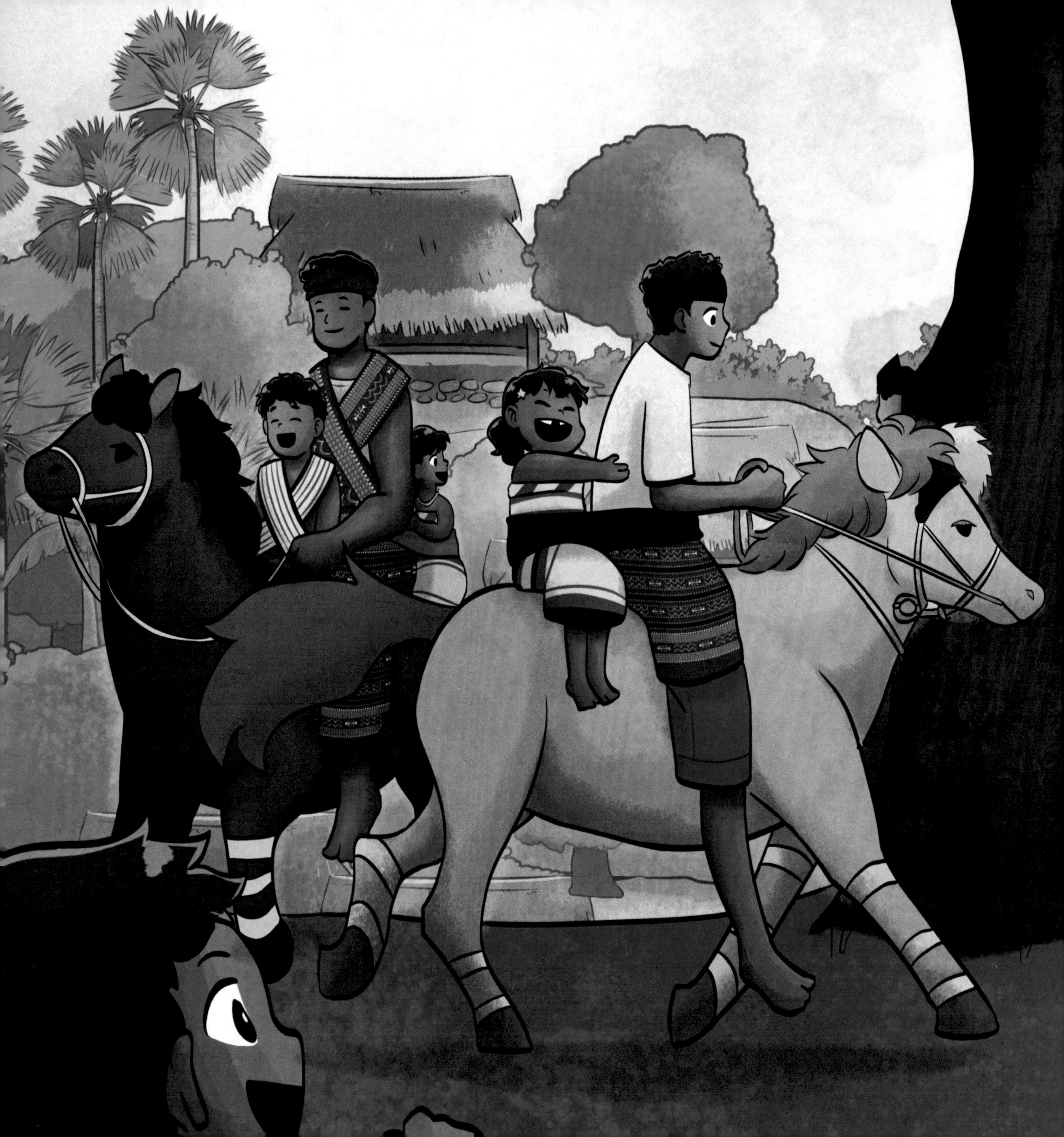

To Mea's joy, the festival didn't last for just one or two days. It continued for seven straight days, and she took part in it all!

On the second day, Mea sat behind a rider performing a horse dance.

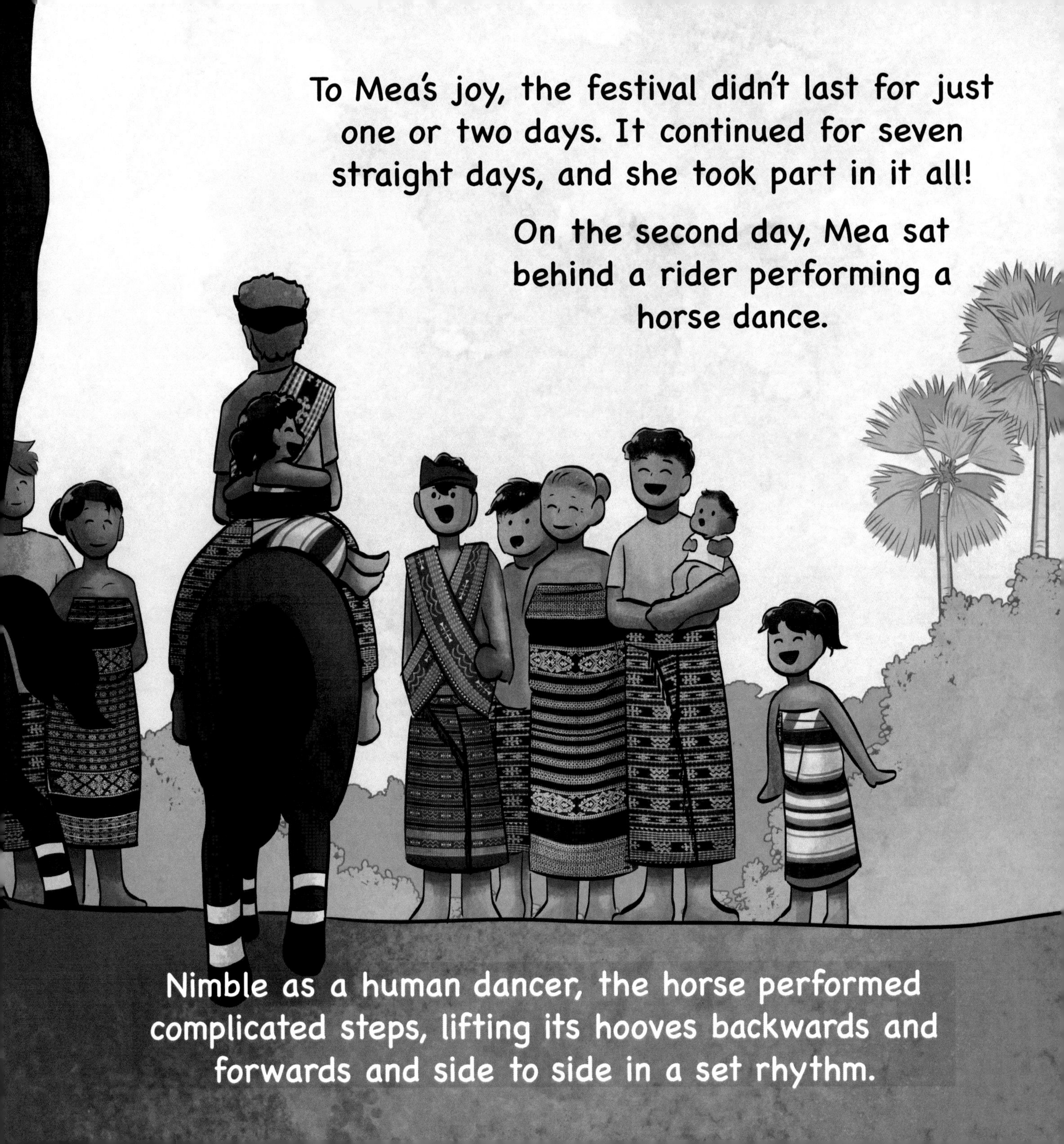

Nimble as a human dancer, the horse performed complicated steps, lifting its hooves backwards and forwards and side to side in a set rhythm.

On the seventh day, the festival closed with a ceremony on the beach. The village priests solemnly planted their swords in the sand.

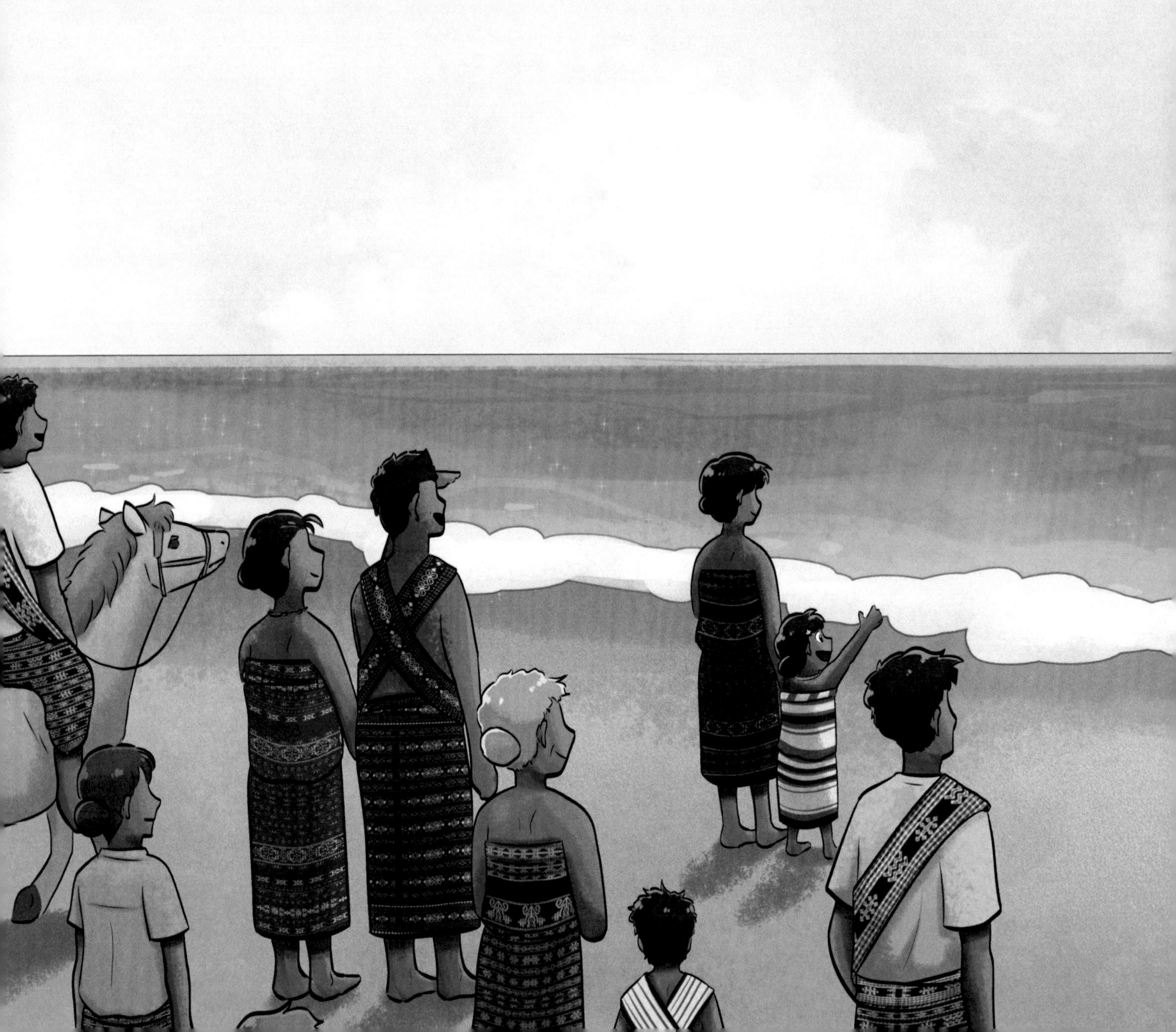

A tiny boat, the *Kowa Holé* boat, was set to float out to sea. It had a beautiful palm leaf sail and was piled with offerings prepared by the villagers for their ancestors.

It was a way of saying "thank you" for the abundant harvest.

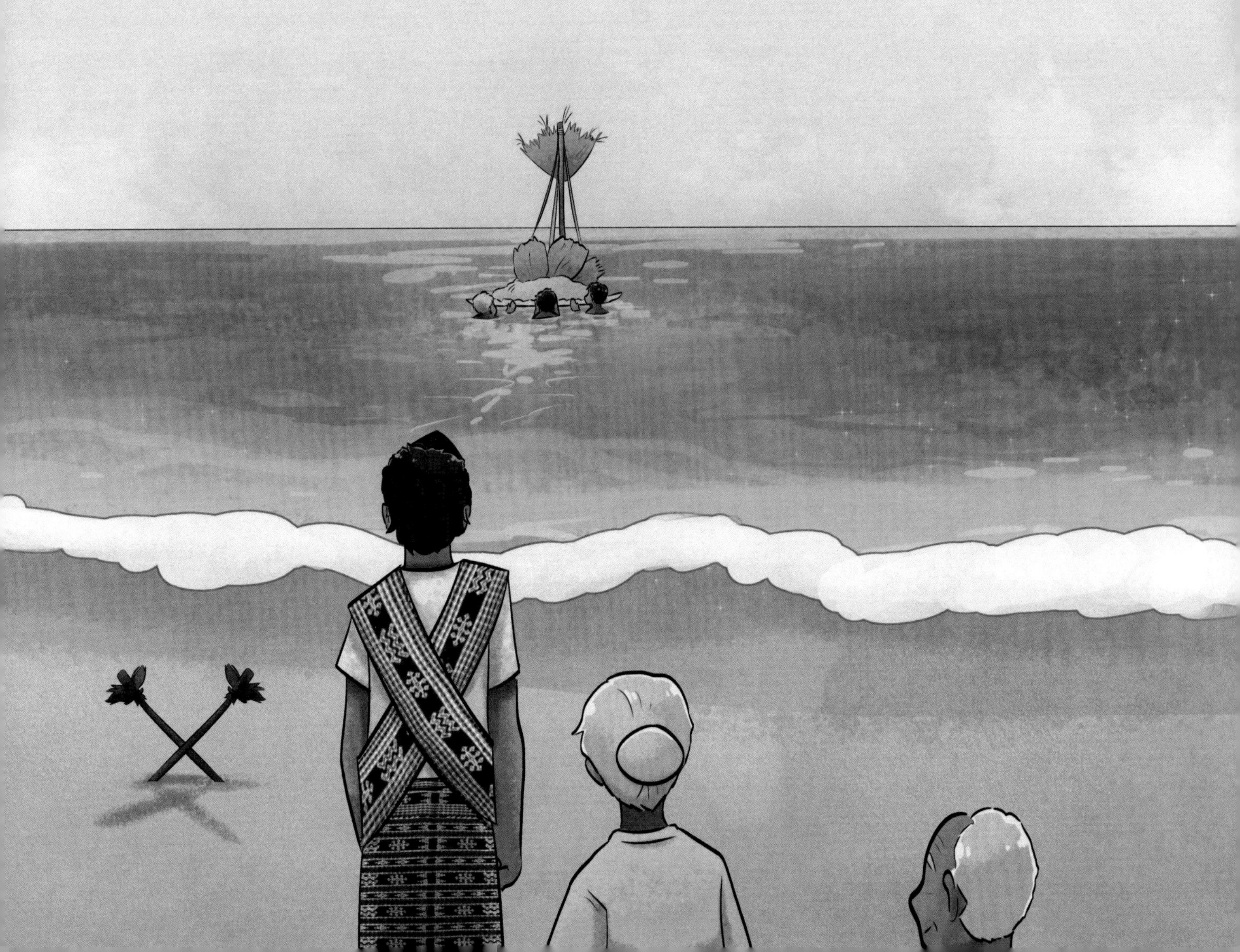

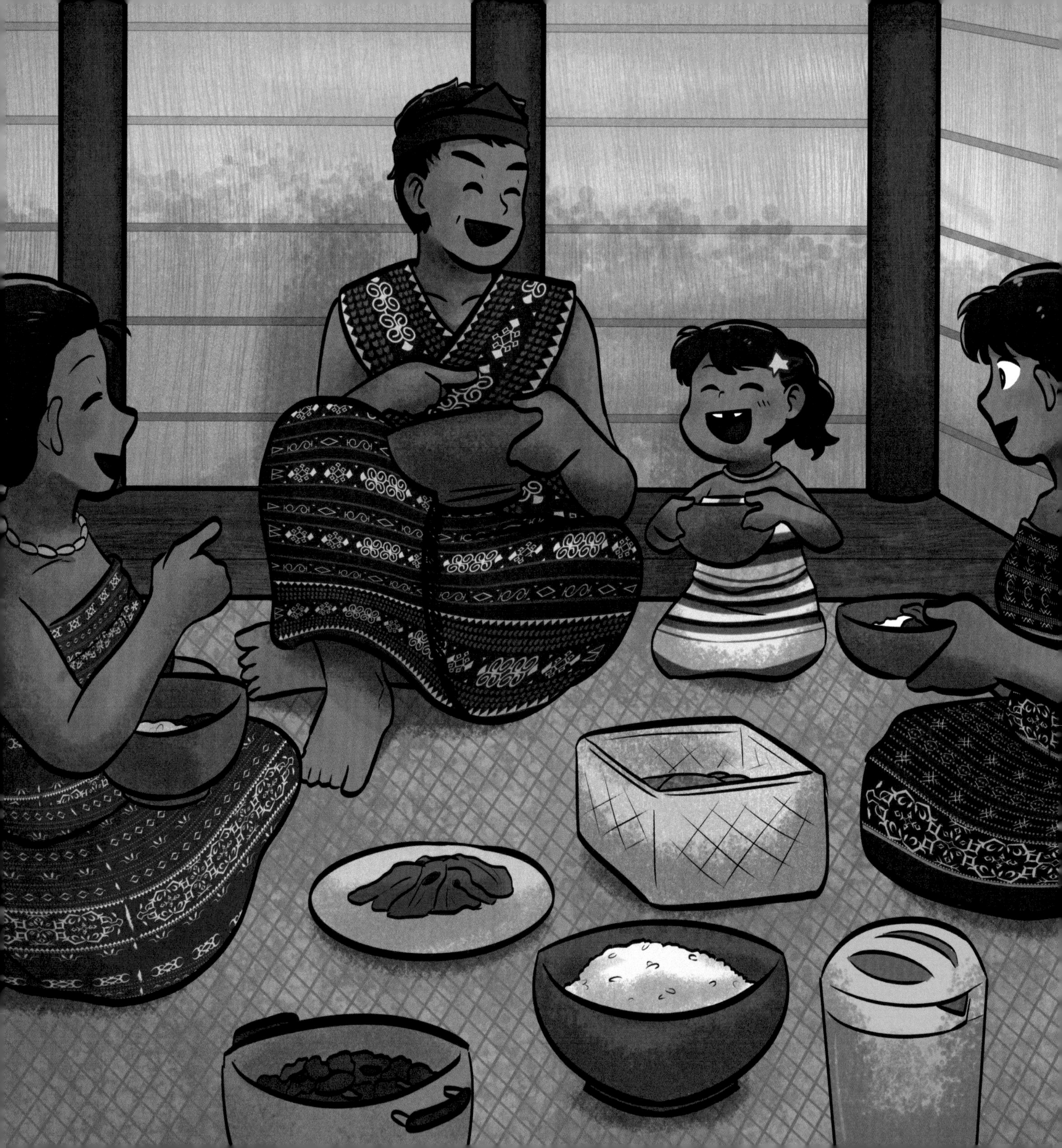

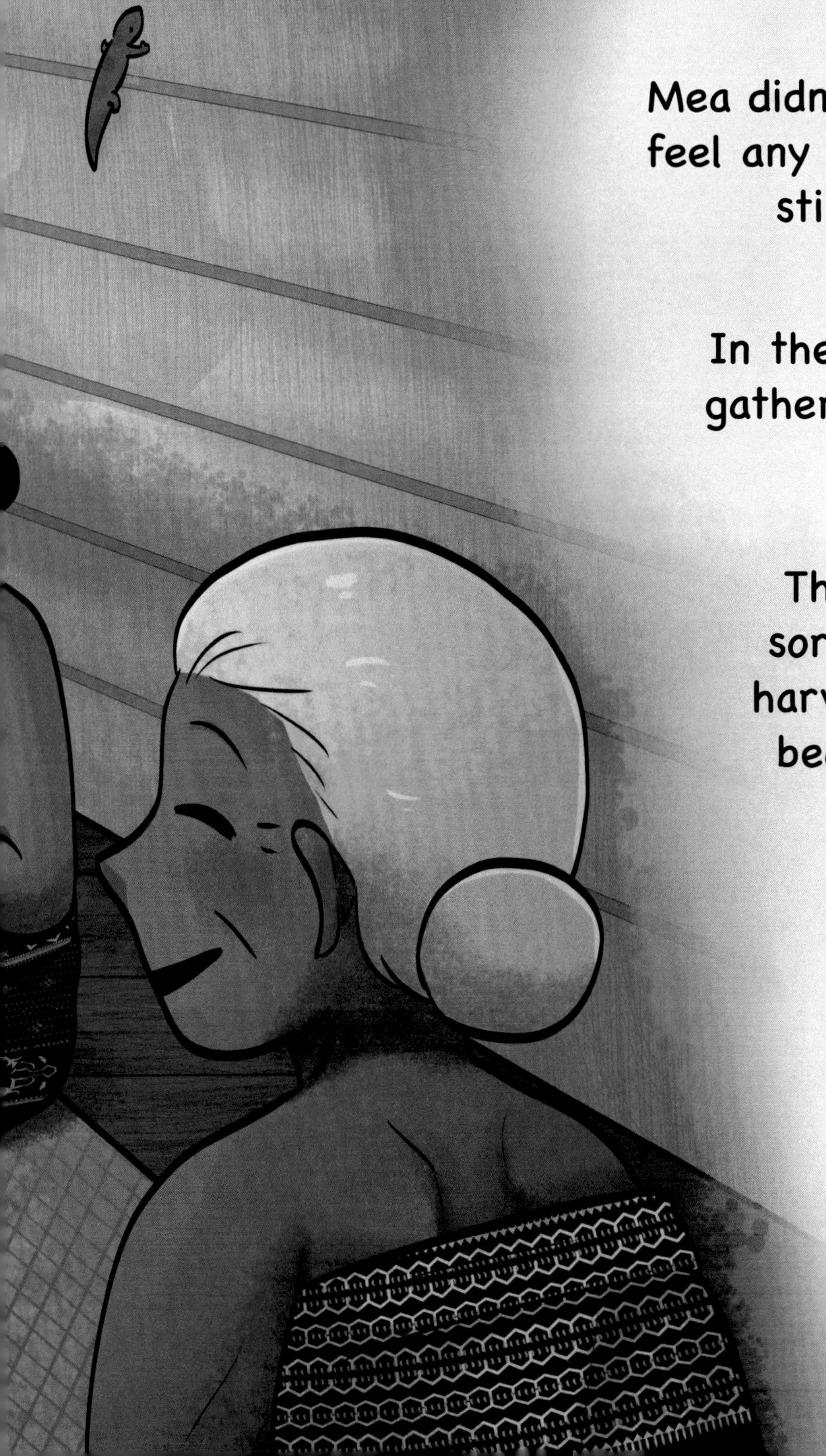

Mea didn't think that she could feel any happier but there was still more to come!

In the evening, her family gathered at Grandmother's house.

They shared rice and sorghum from the new harvest as well as mung beans and palm sugar.

Mea couldn't remember eating a more delicious meal.

At home, there was another surprise. Mother reached for a basket that was resting on top of a cupboard. Mea was puzzled. She didn't recall ever seeing that basket before.

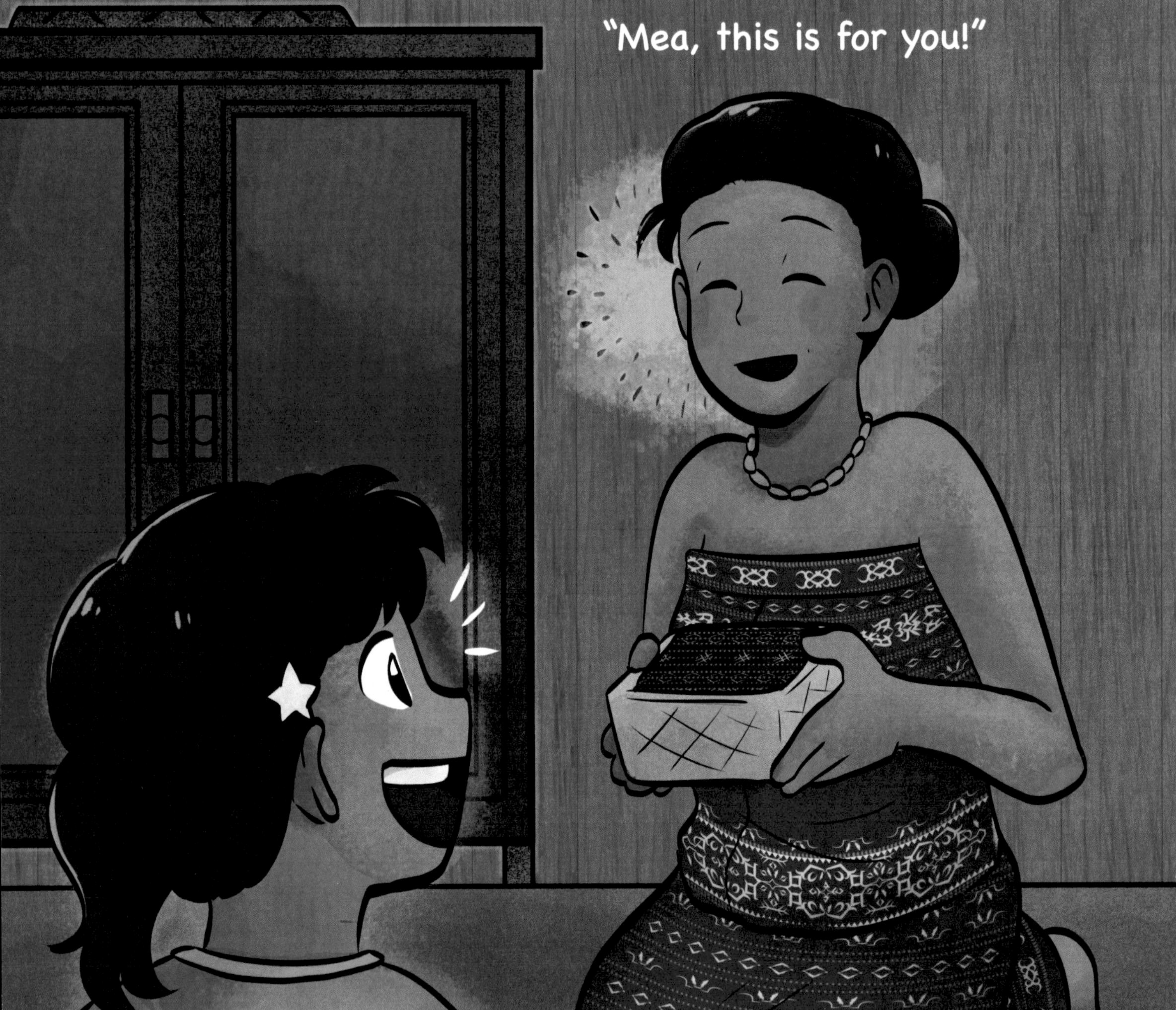
"Mea, this is for you!"

To Mea's wonder, inside the basket was a length of *ikat* sarong, woven with her family's *Patola* pattern!

"This is the other cloth I wove for you," Mother said.

"When you are older, it will be your own family cloth."

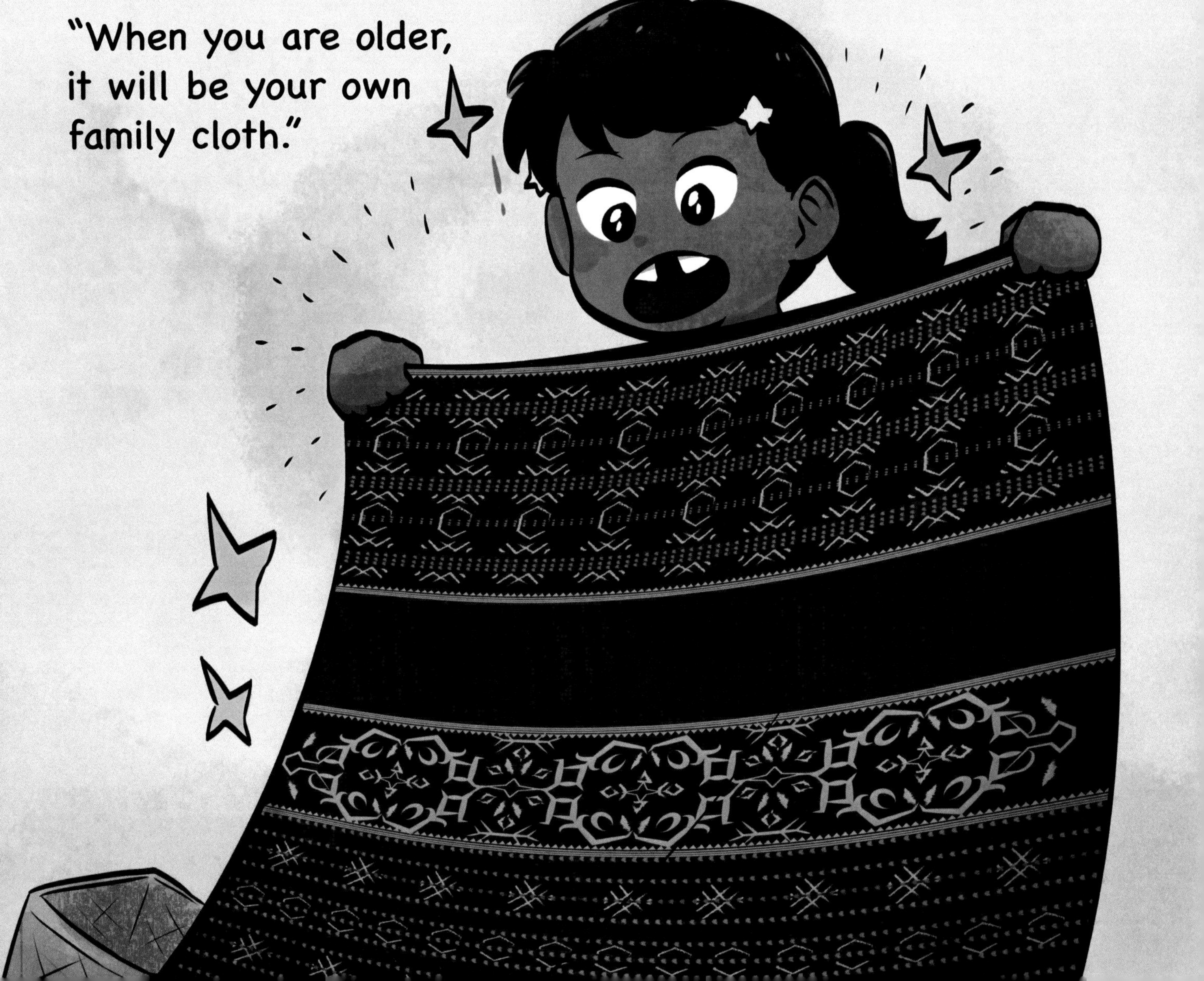

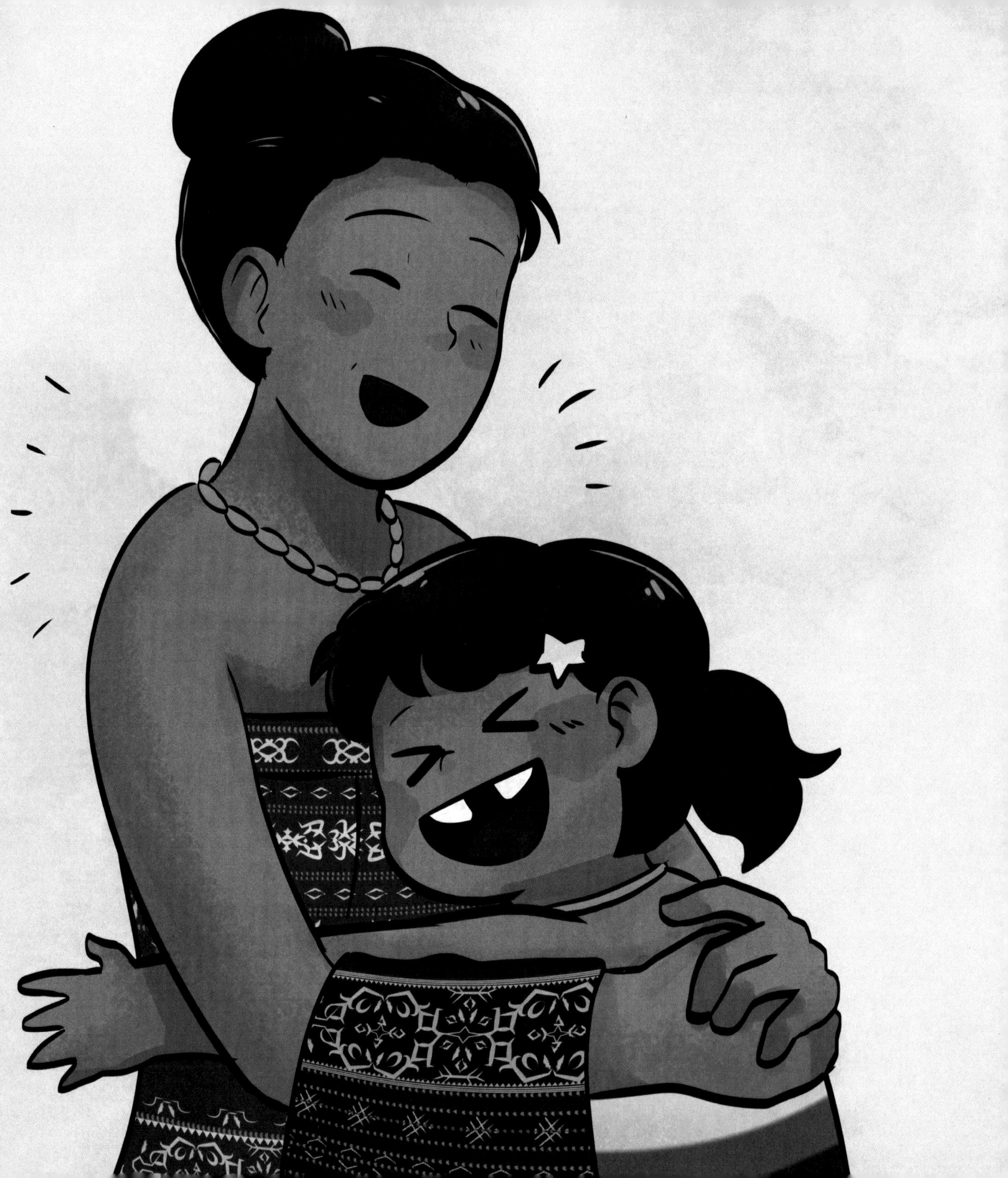

Mea hugged her mother tight.

"Thank you, Ina! It is so pretty! I will cherish it forever!"

"I hope that someday I can weave an *ikat* cloth as beautiful as this."

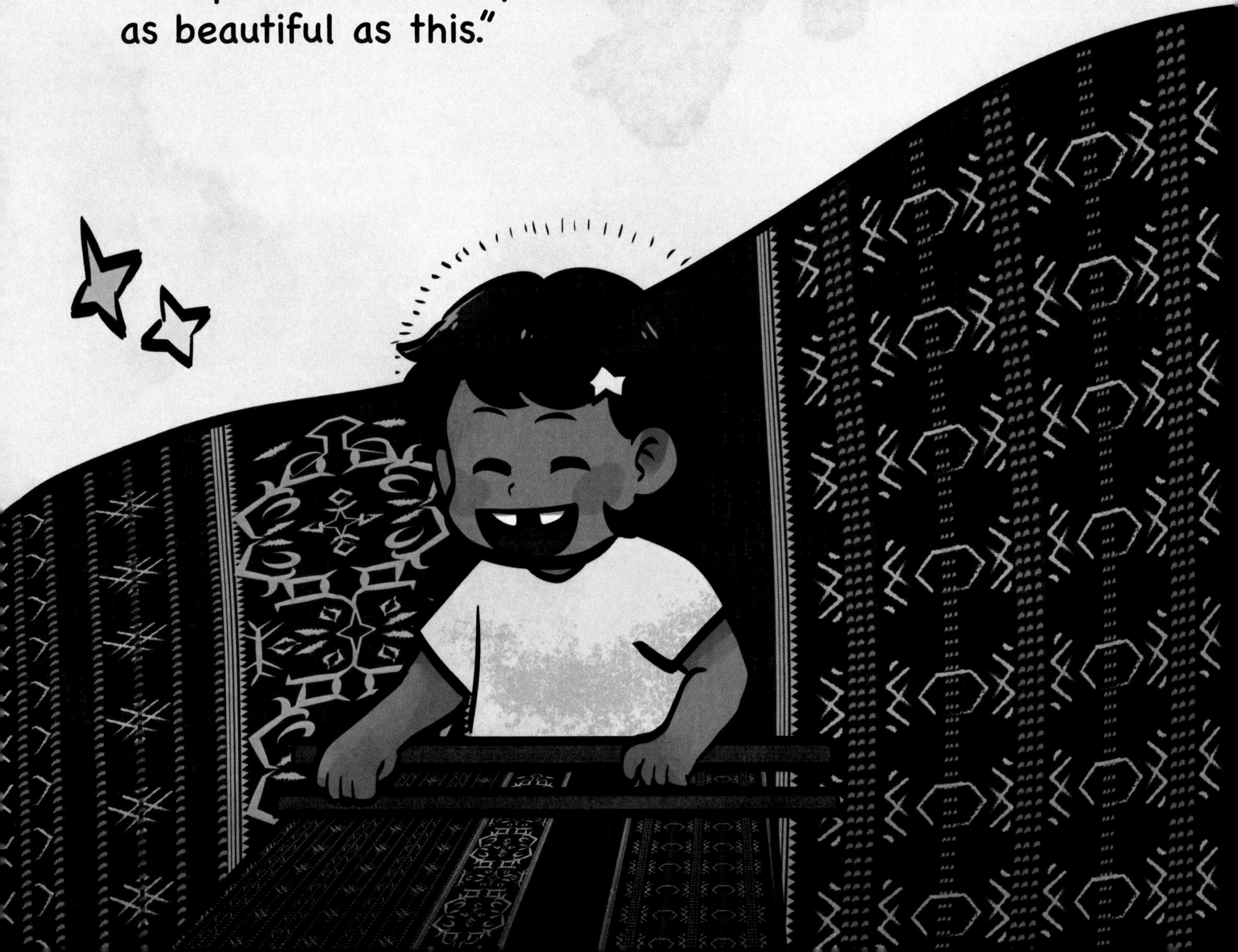

That night, Mea of the Small Palm Flowers slept soundly. Her dreams overflowed with happy images.

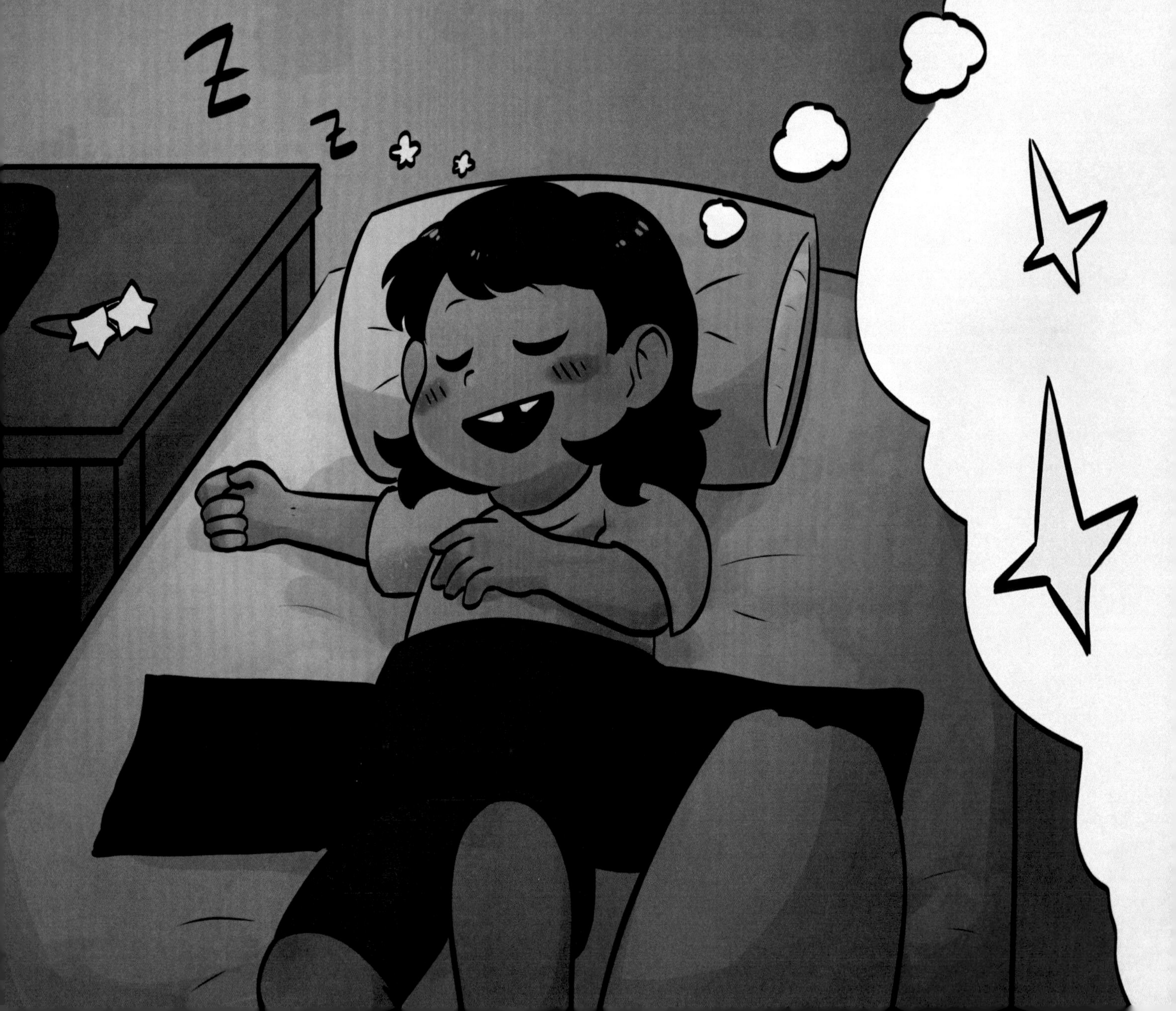

She dreamed of all
the beautiful *ikat* patterns
she saw at the festival.

She dreamed of herself
as a grown up girl
wearing her family's
special *Patola* pattern.

Mea was very happy
and proud to be
one of the Palm Flowers.

Can you find these illustrations in this book of the steps to making an *ikat*?

1. Spinning cotton into threads

2. Tying bundles of threads to make *ikat* patterns

3. Dyeing threads for color

4. Drying threads after dyeing

5. Taking out *ikat* ties to reveal the patterns

6. Weaving an *ikat* cloth

Author: Meirina Soe,
a writer based in Surabaya, Indonesia, who has a special liking for fantasy.
She can be reached at meirinasoewarno@gmail.com.

Illustrator: Wini Boenadhi,
an artist based in Surabaya, Indonesia, who has a passion for comic books.
She can be reached at winonanb@gmail.com.

Cultural Adviser: Ice Tede Dara,
a weaver in Savu Island, who is a member of the Tewuni Rai's woman's
cooperative. Their products can be found at: www.mtmindonesia.com.

Cultural Adviser: Dr. Geneviève Duggan,
an anthropologist and researcher of Savu culture and genealogy.
She can be reached at www.genevieveduggan.com.

Editor: Dr. Sandra Sardjono,
an independent researcher and president of the Tracing Patterns Foundation.

Special Acknowledgment
This book would not have been possible without support from Ice Tede Dara and
Dr. Geneviève Duggan, who have generously shared their rich understanding of
Savu culture. Their field photographs have inspired the illustrations in this book.

ISBN 978-1-7367774-1-1

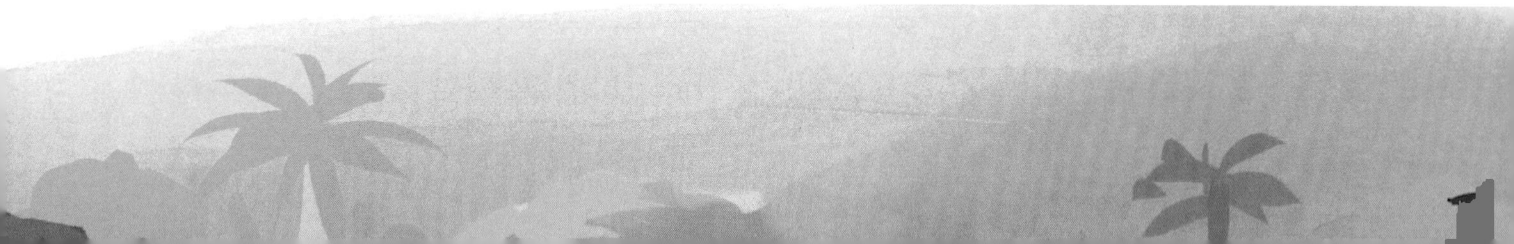